Sail Trim
Theory and Practice

Peter Hahne

ADLARD COLES NAUTICAL

Published by Adlard Coles Nautical
an imprint of A & C Black Publishers Ltd
38 Soho Square, London W1D 3HB
www.adlardcoles.com

First published by Paul Pietsch Verlage GmbH + Co 2001

First UK edition 2005
Reprinted 2007

ISBN 978-0-7136-7225-1

A CIP catalogue record for this book is available from the British Library.

This book is produced using paper that is made from wood grown in
managed, sustainable forests. It is natural, renewable and recyclable. The
logging and manufacturing processes conform to the environmental
regulations of the country of origin.

Typeset in 10/12pt Futura Light
Printed and bound in Singapore by Tien Wah Press Pte Ltd

Note: While all reasonable care has been taken in the production of this
publication, the publisher takes no responsibility for the use of the methods
or products described in the book.

Photographs and diagrams: Peter Hahne apart from:
page 4 Markus Drenckhan, page 36 Ralf G. Weise

Contents

Introduction

ailing a boat is easy. You simply cast off, hoist the sails, then haul in the sheets until they fill and stop flapping. The boat will then gather way and start moving through the water.

What happens afterwards, however, depends largely on sail trim. If you are able to adjust your sails properly, the difference can be dramatic – particularly when sailing to windward – and might even mean reaching a harbour in the evening rather than late at night. Correct sail trim is also important in heavy weather when boats seem to develop minds of their own and you need to stay in control. In light airs too, it's vital to know how to make the sails work efficiently and make use of every last breath; everyone prefers to keep their boat moving rather than having it drift about aimlessly at the whim of tide and current. Above all, sail trim can be adapted, not just to match prevailing conditions, but to suit individual needs. Racing skippers, for example, generally trim their sails to make their boats go as fast as they possibly can. Cruising skippers, on the other hand, may much prefer to potter – in which case, knowing how to trim the sails correctly will make the

experience even more enjoyable. But beyond all that, an understanding of sail trim is a fundamental part of boat handling, and to that extent, a positive safety factor at sea.

Allow me to describe, as briefly as possible, a practical example which I feel underlines the point. I learnt the basics of sailing from a friend who knew how to steer a boat while he was still in short trousers. Many years ago, we borrowed a small sailing cruiser and set off for the day. To start with, it was warm and sunny but gradually, as the day wore on, it got hotter and hotter.

With clouds gathering overhead, and as we drifted in a total calm, my friend told me what to do. We needed to change the genoa and set the storm jib, move the jib fairleads further forward, double-reef the main, and generally tighten all the halyards and sheets. Finally, my friend tensioned the adjustable backstay until the mast had a pronounced curve. After that, he calmly sat by the tiller and waited.

Soon, the thunderstorm arrived. Shortly afterwards, gale-force winds hit us with terrific force. My friend eased the sheets and bore away on a beam reach. While chaos erupted on the other boats around us – with crews trying hard to control wildly flapping sails – our boat merely heeled over a few degrees and raced off gracefully in a cloud of white spray.

To our disappointment, we could only enjoy this exhilarating sailing for about an hour, after which the thunderstorm passed on and the wind died down again. But the experience taught me a lot. I was also so impressed that I desperately wanted to know more about the theory and practice of sail trim. I've not become a racing man, but even as a cruising skipper I still like getting the best out of my boat.

Having said that, I don't like simply learning rules but prefer to understand what I'm meant to be doing. I don't think I could ever blindly follow instructions like a cooking recipe. But

once I grasped how a sailing boat harnesses energy from the wind to drive it along, and how the sails and the keel or centreboard actually work, I was less confused by the numerous control lines. Sail trim suddenly became self-explanatory and fascinating, because I had a better understanding of the big picture.

On the following pages, I shall try to show you my way of achieving correct sail trim. And as long as you don't ignore the theoretical part at the beginning, you won't ever have to learn sail trim rules by heart.

Incidentally, if you're a beginner, some of the technical terms may be new to you. To make it all easier to understand, I've included a small glossary at the back.

Peter Hahne

► *Learning how to trim your sails correctly will make sailing much more enjoyable.*

A little sailing theory

S ail trim is the art of adjusting a sail so it takes up the correct profile at the optimum angle to the wind. That doesn't get us very far because we need a definition of words like 'correct' and 'optimum'. Perhaps we should say that the trim of the sails is correct when the boat is sailing as well as it possibly can in a given set of circumstances – by which we mean the sea state and strength of wind. To achieve this happy state of affairs, the profile and the angle of the sails must provide the best balance between lift and resistance when sailing a particular course, in particular conditions.

But this statement is still vague and begs even more questions. For example, where do lift and resistance come from? What exactly do they do, and when would the best balance between the two actually be achieved? To find out, we must undertake a brief trip into the world of hydrodynamics and aerodynamics. Although water is liquid and air is a mixture of gases, they both act similarly when we analyse the way they flow. The primary difference is their different densities. However, we can see the main flow characteristics of both mediums by looking at water.

Note: When I use the terms 'windward' and 'leeward' in this chapter, they refer to the flow of the individual medium, which in this case is water. Don't think of them as conventional sailing terms! Windward here simply means the side of the body angled towards the flow; leeward is the side of the body away from the flow.

Laminar and turbulent flows

An important physical characteristic of water is its viscosity, which might also be described as a measure of its tenacity. Water consists of tiny little particles, which, as everyone knows, consist of H_2O molecules, in which two hydrogen atoms are bound to one oxygen atom. Certain forces are associated with these molecules, which, in practice, are interactions that make them stick together. If water flows past a solid body, it parts and flows around the external contours. In the border-area, the water molecules not only stick together, but also enter into an interaction with the surface of the solid body. Imagine that this border area consists of several very thin layers of water. Each of the layers is only one molecule thick. The first

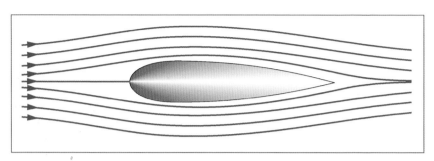

▲ *A laminar flow around the contours of a smooth object.*

layer will stick to the solid surface and remain still. The second layer is one molecule away from the surface of the object, and so, rather than sticking to it, will move along very slowly over the first layer. Above that is a third layer, which will flow a little faster, and a fourth, moving faster still, and a fifth, and so on, until the molecules in this border-area end up flowing as fast as all the other molecules in the surrounding water. This kind of flow, where the particles flow neatly in layers, and in the same direction, is called *laminar*. The contour of a body surrounded by water flowing past in a laminar way will divert the flow from its original direction.

If the flow is extremely fast or if the contour of the body forces it to change direction dramatically, the interaction between water and body may not be sufficiently strong to allow the water to flow past the body in a laminar way: the flow breaks away or 'tears off' and becomes turbulent.

▲ *Where the flow breaks away, it becomes turbulent.*

This means it's disturbed behind the point where it breaks away from the body. The water molecules won't flow in the same direction any more, but rather dance around chaotically in all directions. The water flowing in a mountain stream for example is turbulent, whirling around every rock and anything else that gets in its way.

Circulation

To better understand how an object reacts in a medium like air or water, we need to construct a model. Fortunately, we don't need expensive computers or fantastically sophisticated equipment to reveal some of the major forces and influences at work here, so let's get started. We take a small board and place it in a stream of water in such a way that the flow is parallel to its surface which, in turn, creates what we call a layered or more commonly a laminar flow. If you now turn the board by only a few degrees against the stream, the flow along the board will still remain essentially laminar. Having said that, the water-flow itself will separate a fair distance away from the board's leading edge and its direction will be diverted so it flows along both sides of the board at the same time. The spot where the flow separates is called the *stagnation point*.

This stagnation point is actually slightly to windward of the board, so the flow has a shorter distance to cover to windward than it has to leeward. The windward flow arrives earlier at the after end – at the break away or tear-off edge – than the leeward flow. For that reason, the two streams will fail to re-unite exactly at the tear-off edge, but the windward flow will curl around it against the main flow. The after stagnation point, which is where the windward and leeward flows re-unite, is therefore located off the tear-off edge to leeward. The flow around the edge creates a small eddy called the *starter* or *initial vortex*. Like every circular motion this vortex has an angular momentum.

There's a natural law in physics which says that in a closed system, without the influx of external influences, the sum of all the angular movements or momentums always remains the same. It's a question of balancing out the forces, if you like. You've only to look at the natural world to see how it works in practice. For example, take a cat that falls from a tree. It never lands on its back because it instinctively rotates its tail as soon as it falls to prevent it from turning upside-down. The angular momentum of its falling body gets corrected by the angular momentum of its tail, so the cat always lands on its paws. A circular motion in a closed system always creates another circular motion but in the opposite direction, so the sum of the momentums remains constant.

What holds good for cats also applies to machines. So, in much the same way, a helicopter has to create an opposing momentum with a small

▲ *In a closed system, the sum of all the moving angles remains constant.*

tail rotor, which compensates the angular momentum of the main rotor. Otherwise, the fuselage of the heli-copter would turn in circles, in the opposite direction. In our experiment, the small board is a closed system with the water flowing past. The initial or starter vortex as described above must therefore create a second eddy whose momentum is equally strong but in the opposite direction. This eddy is called the *circulation*. The initial or starter vortex is rather like a small cogwheel that drives another, larger wheel.

The circulation embraces the entire board and runs with the original flow to leeward and against the original flow to windward. Unfortunately, the circulation is impossible to detect because it superimposes itself on the

original flow. As a result, all we can see is an accelerated flow to leeward and a slower flow to windward. To leeward, the circulation runs with the flow and thus accelerates; to wind-ward it runs against the flow and slows it down. If you want to see the starter vortex and resulting flows, you can conduct a simple experiment in your bath. All you need to do is just simply pour a handful of fine sawdust into the water and place a small board about half way along. Once the surface of the water has settled and is completely still, pull the board through the water, which stimulates the flow, at an angle of two or three degrees.

As soon as you begin to move the board, a small but significant eddy

▶ *If you pull a flat board through the water, and angle it a few degrees against the stream, a small eddy forms at the back edge where the flow tears off. This is the starter vortex.*

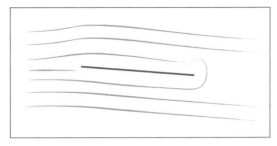

will form at the after end (the tear-off edge) and will remain in place as you move the board away. As you can see, the starter vortex doesn't stick to the tear-off edge, but moves away from it with the flow. As soon as the starter vortex has set the circulation in motion, the faster flow along the lee side will reach the tear-off edge at the same time as the now slower windward flow. These two flows can now reunite without further disturbance or eddies at the after end of the board. If you look very closely, you will see that the sawdust along the lee side, which in this instance is the side away from the direction in which you pull the board, will indeed flow faster than that along the windward side.

Now, at the end of your bath, quickly pull the board out of the water and you'll notice that another, larger eddy will form which again runs in the opposite direction to the smaller starter vortex. This is the circulation again that becomes visible once you've cut off the overriding horizontal flow by pulling the board up out of the water.

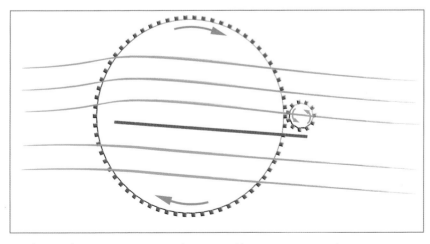

▲ *The initial vortex triggers a circular motion, like a cog in a gear-box.*

The creation and duration of the circulation is entirely dependent on the laminar flow. If the angle which the board in your bath makes against the flow is too large, the laminar flow will tear off at a certain point. When that happens, the laminar flow will then become turbulent and the circulation will stop.

Lift and resistance

Our experiment in the bath also shows something else; it may seem obvious enough but, in fact, as we shall see, will prove highly significant. Not surprisingly perhaps, it takes more effort to pull the board at a small angle through the water, than merely keeping it in line with the flow. At the same time you'll feel an influence or force that tries to squeeze the board off-course towards the lee side. So what do you do in order to avoid a premature collision with the side of the bath? You have to take avoiding action and pull the board not only forward, but also slightly to windward – and that means exerting two forces at the same time: one forward to overcome the resistance of the water and get the board moving, and the other one slightly to windward to counteract any tendency to drift off to leeward. This simple experiment goes to the very heart of what makes a boat sail at different angles to the wind.

But, even if, as we've already admitted, the effect seems obvious, where exactly does this force to leeward come from? We've seen that the circulation accelerates the flow to leeward and slows it down to windward. Similarly, the pressure is lower in a faster flow than it is in a slower one. This means that the circulation

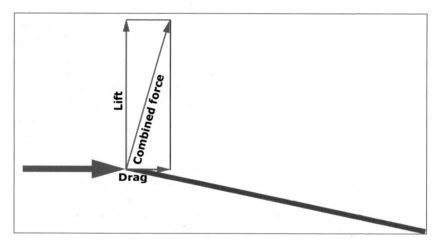

▲ The difference in pressures on the windward and leeward sides creates a combined force that can be broken down into two components: lift and drag.

effectively reduces the pressure along the leeside and increases it to windward. The difference in pressure results in a force that will always try to 'suck' the board to leeward. It can be divided into two components: the *lift*, which works at a right-angle to the flow directly to leeward, and the *resistance*, which works in the direction of the flow and has the effect of a brake.

The resistance has several origins:

- The *viscosity*, or thickness, of the water molecules allows them to 'stick' to the surface of the moving body. These particles will try to pull the board along in the direction of the general flow. They create a friction that forms the largest component of the overall resistance.
- The form of the board – whether it's thick or thin; whether the leading edge is rounded or not, and so on – will slow the flow down, and is called the *flowing resistance*. Mathematically, this resistance grows with the square of the speed of the flow. If the speed of the flow is doubled, the resistance quadruples.
- Because the flowing water has to give way to the shape of the board, waves are created on the surface of the water. The energy needed to create them is taken from the energy that drives the board through the water. The waves also slow the board down. This is called the *wave resistance*.

- Finally, the difference in pressure between the leeward and windward sides of the board results in water flowing beneath the bottom edge – the foot of the board – from windward to leeward. This flow creates turbulence which, in turn also uses up energy. This is called *induced resistance*.
- All these single factors are generally grouped together under the term 'form resistance'.

Lift and resistance alter with the angle of the board towards the flow. In practice, the amount of resistance grows continuously as the angle is increased. As long as the angle is small, say, not more than perhaps three or four degrees, the resistance increases only relatively slowly. Even if the flow is still laminar along the sides, the resistance will grow as the angle increases. And if the board is angled at more than about ten degrees, the flow will begin to tear off and the resistance will rapidly increase. Maximum resistance is reached at a point when the board is at right angles to the flow.

In contrast, the lifting force only improves and grows with an ever increasing angle and as long as the flow remains laminar. At the beginning, it grows quicker than the resistance. Maximum lift is reached at the point just before the laminar flow begins to break away and tear off. But even before that, the relative values of lift and resistance will soon begin to change.

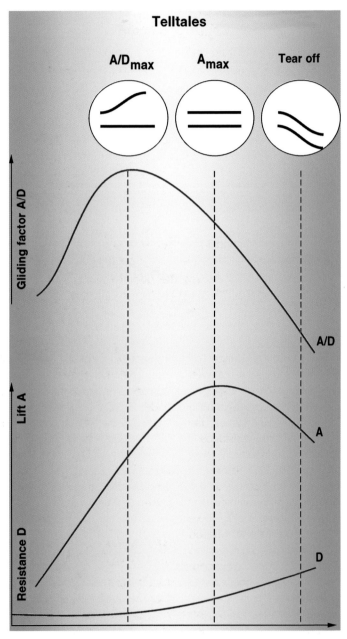

▲ *Only when the angle to the flow is small does lift increase more quickly than drag.*

FACT BOX

So far we've only been looking at the effects of a board in the water rather than sails in the wind; even so, we can still draw some interesting and relevant conclusions:

Rule
When sailing upwind, it's not the angle to the wind which delivers the maximum lift that matters; what you really want to find is the angle that gives the best relationship between lift and drag. The optimum angle provides maximum lift with minimum drag. A smaller angle would create less drag, but also less lift. A larger angle would certainly create more lift but would be offset by increased drag.

Exceptions
Of course, there may be conditions at sea when you need maximum lift, in which case an increase in drag is simply a price you have to pay. By the same token, in other circumstances, the priorities might be different; you might want to reduce drag, for example, even if that means ending up with limited lift. We shall look at these trade-offs more closely later on.

To be precise, the resistance will quickly become stronger than the lift. This means that there's one specific angle where the lift may not yet have reached its peak, but where the relation between lift and resistance is at its optimum. This is reached when the quotient of lift and resistance is high – which means achieving the best possible lift with the minimum of resistance – or to put it slightly more mathematically, when the lift divided by the resistance produces a relatively high number. This particular number or quotient is called the *gliding factor*.

As you might have guessed, the term 'gliding factor' has been stolen from aviation technology. The higher the gliding factor of an aircraft's wing

– which means the more lift it creates with the lowest possible resistance – the further the plane will be able to glide without any propulsion other than gravity which, of course, enables it to glide towards the ground.

Perhaps having considered baths and aircraft, we should now look at how lift and resistance – or drag – is generated by a sail.

Lift and drag in a sail

As already intimated, water and air work in similar ways. That's why a sail which has been sheeted in towards the wind will create the same flow phenomena as the slightly angled board which we used in our experiment in the bath. The fact that the flow media in this case is air, or a mixture of gases, rather than water, makes little difference. In terms of flow properties, gases have much the same principal characteristics as water; the two mediums only differ in their respective densities. In this context, and if it helps, you could also consider air as a particularly thin and dry form of water. In other words it's reasonable to compare hydro-dynamics and aerodynamics – at least assuming the speed of the flow remains fairly low.

As you sheet in a flapping sail, you set it at an angle to the wind, which we should now think of as the flowing medium. The sail now basically acts in exactly the same way as the small board that we pulled along through the water in our bath. Just off the luff and slightly to windward of it, the flow separates. It then flows along the sail on both sides and re-unites just before the leech on the leeward side. This is where, immediately upon sheeting in the sail, the initial or starter vortex will form and set the circulation in motion. This slows down the flow to wind-ward and increases the speed of the flow to leeward. As a result, pressure is increased to windward and decreased to leeward.

This difference in pressure creates an overall aerodynamic force that can be separated into lift and drag. You can, however, also separate it into two forces that are far more practical and meaningful for small boat skippers: the *driving force* and the *heeling force*.

The driving force moves the boat along while the heeling force pushes it over on its side. The heeling force also encourages a slight difference between the centreline of the boat and the course steered – the so-called *leeway factor*. In practice, therefore, the actual course sailed will differ by a few degrees from the direction in

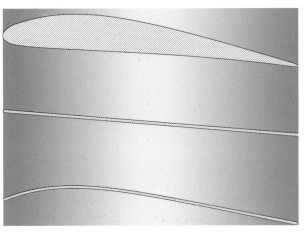

◀ *An aircraft wing, a board and a sail all have significantly different profiles.*

FACT BOX

Despite their different profiles, all three objects: board, sail and wing, produce lift. As a matter of fact, it's not the actual shape that's responsible for the basic phenomenon – though it's true that different profiles create different amounts of lift and drag. What a skipper needs to know when trying to get the best from his boat is that the relation between lift and drag is dependent on the angle to the flow and the profile of the sail.

which the helmsman may be pointing the bows of the boat.

These phenomena were originally the subject of scientific research when scientists were working on aircraft development. The board in the bath, along with the sail of your boat, may also be referred to as a 'wing' because both act in the same way as an aircraft wing. However, the lift of the aircraft wing acts in a vertical direction, forcing the aircraft up and keeping it in the air, while the lift of the board and the sail acts in horizontal direction, 'sucking' it to leeward. In the same way, and not surprisingly, the term 'gliding factor' which describes the relationship between lift and drag also comes from aviation technology.

The three wings: board, sail and aircraft wing, are different in their respective forms, shapes or profiles. The aircraft wing normally has a more or less pronounced asymmetrical profile with a rounded leading edge, a strongly curved, concave upper side and a straight or slightly convex lower side. Towards the trailing edge, the wing profile becomes considerably straighter and thinner.

The board has a completely symmetrical profile with a square leading edge and an equally square trailing edge. It's thin and straight. A profile like this is called 'overly critical'.

The sail is similar in profile to the aircraft wing, but with one all important difference: it's thin – much thinner even than the board. The wing's rounded profile also remains exactly the same to windward and leeward at every point – whereas a sail's profile can easily be changed by adjusting a few simple controls.

Forces above and below the water

A sailing boat can sail 'against' the wind because part of its hull is immersed in water which creates a resistance that hinders it from drifting away to leeward. This resisting force creates the forward drive that moves it along its desired course. As the underwater parts of the boat pass through the water, which in turn flows around the hull and its appendages, we can assume that yet another 'wing' is at work here.

Let's take a look at a sailing dinghy. It sails nearly upright with a centreboard protruding downwards into the water. If the centreboard were to be lifted out of the water, the boat would immediately begin to drift away to leeward. Only with the centreboard back in the water can the boat again be steered at an angle to the wind, rather than finding itself blown along in the same direction. The centreboard of a racing dinghy is usually rather deep and narrow, with a long leading edge, and a slightly rounded, symmetrical profile.

One might now assume that the centreboard would simply create lateral resistance and resist the tendency to drift off to leeward, thus forcing the boat on course. But when you look at the relatively small area of the centreboard, the argument is less convincing. And if the boat is deliberately slowed down by sheeting in the sails extremely hard, it will again begin to drift to leeward.

Clearly, the total area of the underwater appendages of the boat (its lateral cross-section) which creates the resistance against leeward drift, won't change with the speed of the boat. What's more important is the speed of the water as it flows past these appendages. From a certain point onwards, the centreboard acts like the wing of an aircraft. If the flow past it is sufficiently fast, the centreboard creates a hydrodynamic force

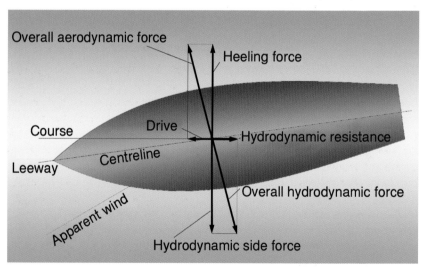

▲ The way a boat behaves is basically a function of balancing forces which get disturbed or upset, then reassert themselves. So, if the overall aerodynamic and hydrodynamic forces are equal, the boat will sail along at a steady angle of heel and at a constant speed. If the wind increases, the boat will heel over and accelerate until, once again, the forces below the water are in balance with those above.

that prevents the boat from drifting to leeward and thus makes sailing to windward possible. However, a wing has to be positioned at a certain angle to the flow to create lift. A sail can be sheeted in such a way that the wind hits it at an angle. A centreboard, in contrast, can be pulled out of the water and lowered back into it, but its direction relative to the flow is fixed. So how can it act like a wing?

If you take a close look at the movements of a dinghy sailing upwind, you'll quickly realise that the actual sailed course will differ from the centreline of the boat by a few degrees. This small angle is called the leeway and is created by the heeling forces already described above. Typical leeway might be between three and six degrees and since the centreboard is normally aligned with the centreline of the boat, the flow will hit it at exactly the same angle. We now have the same phenomenon as we did with the aircraft wing. An initial vortex is created at the aft tearing-off edge and the circulation that creates the lift is set in motion.

As with the sails, the different speeds of the flow to windward and to leeward of the centreboard create a hydrodynamic force that can be broken down into the hydrodynamic resistance and the hydrodynamic side force. These forces above and below the water interact with each other. The hydrodynamic side force acts in opposition to the aerodynamic

heeling force, and the hydrodynamic resistance works against the aerodynamic forward force. If these forces acting on the centreboard and the sails are equally strong, the boat will sail to windward at a constant angle of heel, making constant leeway and a constant speed. On a yacht, the keel replaces the centreboard and has three main functions. It carries ballast and places the centre of gravity as low as possible, thereby increasing stability. With its lateral area, it dampens rolling in a seaway and finally, it creates the hydrodynamic side force which, as we've seen, is the key factor which enables a boat to sail close to the wind.

Wing profiles

Research in wind-tunnels has shown that while the profile of a wing is not in itself the reason why it creates lift, it does greatly influence the relation between lift and resistance. A bulging profile, as opposed to a slim and straight one, will create more lift but at the same time more resistance. Conversely, a slim and straight profile, may not create as much lift but will meet with less resistance. Similarly, the positioning of the bulge is important. If the profile has its deepest bulge at a point about 45 percent of the profile's width aft of the leading edge, the lift will be substantial. On the other hand, the flow may tear off too early immediately behind the bulge if it moves too

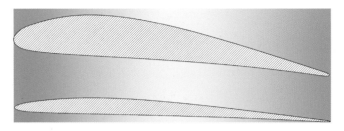

◀ A deep, baggy profile creates more lift; a slim profile has less drag.

quickly. That would be less of a problem with a slimmer profile whose main bulge might be located, say, about 35 percent of the way behind the leading edge.

A wing whose tear-off edge takes the form of an elliptical curve has the effect of encouraging a good relationship between lift and drag; in other words it will develop more lift and less drag.

A wing with a long leading edge and a short base will create considerably more lift than one with a short leading edge and a wide base. Such a short and fat wing will induce more resistance because of the stronger compensation of pressure along its wide base. This compensating flow around the base can be reduced by fitting a small profile horizontally on the wing itself. Many aircraft wings have these so-called winglets fixed on the ends of their wings which dramatically reduce induced resistance.

Similarly, wings fitted at the lower ends of some modern fin keels are effectively doing the same job as winglets and have usually been adopted in an attempt to reduce the induced resistance created by the flow around the lower edge of the keel.

Of course, it's impossible to fit winglets or anything like them to soft, crinkly sails. However, we sometimes see deck-sweeping genoas where the tack and the clew are cut so low that the foot of the sail actually touches the deck. Here, the deck stops the flow around the foot of the sail and again reduces any induced resistance. In practice, deck-sweepers may have obvious theoretical advantages but are unwieldy, especially on long beats to windward when you need to make lots of short tacks.

Since wings don't always work well in different environments, it seems reasonable to suppose that it might be useful if their profiles could be adjusted to match particular conditions. As we all know, the rigid profiles of aircraft wings can only be adjusted by using a rather complex system of flaps. Pilots use them on take-off and landing, for example, to change the profile and make it more or less pronounced. During take-off the plane would still be moving fairly slowly and need to create maximum lift. Conversely while landing, a deep profile creating maximum drag would be more important. Extra resistance would also be required here to slow the plane down to touch-down

▶ *Sails with a long leading edge and a short base, as well as an elliptical leech, are particularly effective upwind.*

speed. But when the aircraft is cruising along at its normal altitude, at its normal speed, resistance should be as low as possible so a slim profile is needed. Sufficient lift would be generated as a result of the higher speed.

A yacht's sail is made of flexible cloth rather than rigid material so its profile and shape is created by the cut of the sail. The sail-maker will cut the sail in such a way that it's not as flat as a tablecloth, but has a three-dimensional form when suspended in the wind. The profile of a sail might be easier to change, but the adjustments themselves are less precise than those on an aircraft wing. Consequently, the stiffer the sail cloth, the easier it is to adjust its profile or trim it to the right angle.

The exact profile of a sail depends on the distribution of the pressure acting on it, which, in turn, is determined by the sheeting angle and the strength of the wind. On the other hand, the form of the sail will also influence the distribution of pressure along its surface.

Normally we have more controls to hand for the trim of the mainsail than we do when we want to trim the headsail. A fractional rig for example means you can control the depth of the mainsail's profile by bending the mast. In a case like this, the sail-maker can cut the mainsail for a bendy mast in such a way that the curve of the luff matches the curve of the mast when it's bent back. When the mast is straight, the additional cloth behind the luff will form a pronounced profile in the sail.

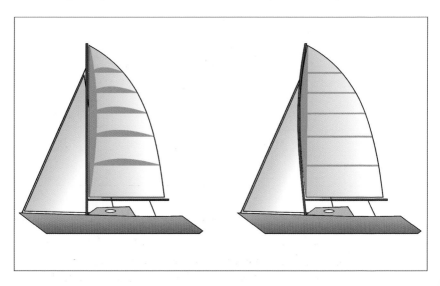

▲ *Bending the mast is a good way of controlling and changing the depth of the profile of the mainsail, assuming it's been cut to allow for such adjustments.*

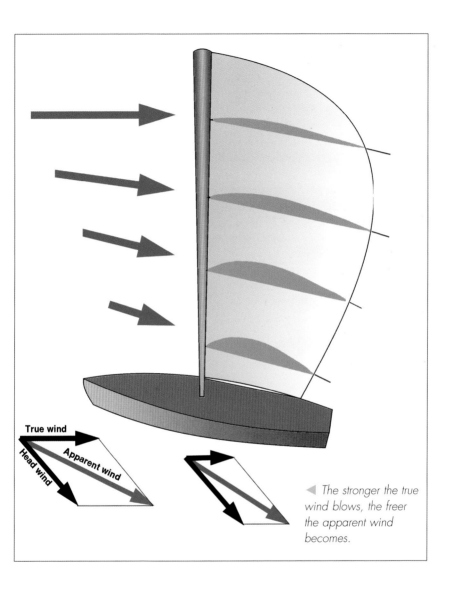

True wind

Head wind

Apparent wind

◀ *The stronger the true wind blows, the freer the apparent wind becomes.*

FACT BOX

The stronger the wind blows, the freer the apparent wind becomes. That's why you can luff up in the gusts and make gains to windward. Racing skippers are particularly good at 'pinching up' to windward.

If the mast is then bent by pulling the backstay tight, its curve will increasingly match the curve of the sail. In that way, the mast will pull the cloth tight and create a much flatter profile.

The three-dimensional form of the sail also takes account of twist. This is you might call the vertical deformation of the sail. To see what it looks like in real life, if you cast your eyes up from the boom along the leech of the mainsail, the amount of twist will be obvious. Another point worth noting is the way the sail seems to open up more and more towards the top. Because of that, the angle of the sail to the wind seems to change from the boom to the top of the mast, but in reality remains constant. The higher it is, the more the wind will change direction. Towards the top of the mast it's much freer than it is at the foot, assuming the boat is moving of course.

If your boat is moored up and stationary, it's impossible to see this change in the direction of the wind. However, the wind will be noticeably stronger at the top of the mast than it is on deck. As long as the boat is moored, you'll be measuring the true wind. This is the atmospheric wind, which is created by the prevailing weather conditions. In a border area some way above the water, the wind gets slowed down by the friction between air and water. The higher up you go the less the friction becomes and the stronger the wind.

Once the boat is underway, the true wind will also be influenced by the head wind. Head wind and true wind come from different directions. The head wind is generated by the speed of the boat and comes from dead ahead; the true wind comes at an angle.

Once a boat is under way, neither the head wind nor the true wind are perceptible as separate entities because they both merge together. We can only measure the overall result which is known as the apparent wind. This is the wind which in effect actually drives the boat along.

But let's take another look at twist. If a sail were prevented from twisting, the angle to the wind could be correctly adjusted at the foot, but at the top of the mast the angle would be too great. That's because the wind would be freer up there. As a result, drive would be lost and the boat would heel more. With the appropriate amount of twist, the angle can be correct from the foot of the sail right up to the top of the mast. This is another important fact.

FACT BOX

The less true wind there is, the more friction there will be along the water. In the same way, the strength of the wind will also increase at higher altitudes. In addition, the wind will be freer the higher it is above the water. That's why it's so important that in light airs, a sail should have more twist than in a light breeze.

Sailing on different courses and angles to the wind

So far, we've only looked at how a sail works when the boat is sailing close-hauled upwind. If a boat sails at a small angle against the predominant flow of air, drive will only be created by the aerodynamic lift of the sail, which in a situation like this acts like an aircraft wing. Aero-dynamic resistance acting in parallel with the incoming wind will slow the boat down. On all upwind courses, we need a lot of lift and as little resistance as possible.

But a boat won't always be sailing upwind. It can sail on a variety of different courses, from a beat to a run. On different points, and at different angles to the wind, the optimum balance between lift and drag changes. As the wind blows

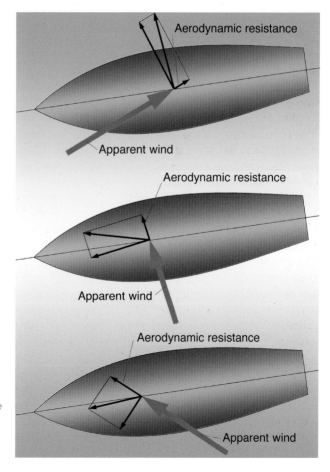

▶ The more aft the wind is, the more aerodynamic drag you get.

more freely, the more it pushes you in the direction that you want to sail, and the more the aerodynamic resistance acts as a positive factor encouraging the boat to move forward in the right direction. It follows, therefore, that a high gliding factor, which means a high quotient of lift against drag, is only desirable when sailing upwind. On a reach, resistance is actually useful because it adds additional momentum to the forward motion. In the same way, once you sail dead downwind, any aerodynamic lift ceases to have any effect at all and the drive is derived solely from aerodynamic resistance. A sailing boat is quickest on courses where lift and drag both contribute to forward drive; which means close reaching. Every boat will be a bit slower close to the wind and dead downwind.

We already know that the gliding factor is dependent on the angle of the sail to the wind as well as its profile. Large angles create more lift but also more drag; once the angle is so large that the flow tears off the sail, only drag is created. Deep, baggy profiles create a lot of lift and a lot of drag.

So while you trim your sails upwind for maximum lift and minimum drag, on a reach everything changes because you want more drag. Upwind, a small angle to the wind and a flat profile is best. On a reach, the angle of the sail towards the wind should become larger and the profile more rounded. Running

dead downwind, the sail should ideally be at an angle of 90 degrees to the wind and have the maximum depth of profile.

In most cases, you won't be able to let out the boom far enough because sooner or later, a shroud will be in the way of the boom. In any case the sail should be trimmed to have a big 'belly' and with a twist that allows the sail to set at right angles to the wind at least from half way up to the top of the mast. But we'll have a closer look at practical sail trim in later chapters.

In spite of the large number of different courses you can sail to the wind, the number of sail trim options are limited. Sails which work effectively upwind, for example, may be hopelessly inefficient in the opposite direction. This was demonstrated particularly dramatically in 1988 by the America's Cup veteran Dennis Conner with his catamaran *Stars and Stripes*. Instead of using a soft sail, he had a boat with an aerodynamically highly effective wing mast with which he could sail at twice the wind speed when going upwind. Downwind however, the catamaran would come to a complete standstill unless he kept gybing so she stayed on a beat. Conversely, sails with a high amount of drag will perform well when running downwind, but poorly when beating upwind. Gaff sails, along with other similar, less triangular configurations, belong in this category. Some blue water sailors swear by gaffs because they generally try to avoid going upwind in the first place, and their primary concern is a decent performance when reaching and running in the Trade Winds. It would be wrong therefore to dismiss traditional rigs out of hand. Many have been developed over generations, largely by trial and error. So while it's unlikely that top racing skippers will ever switch to gaffs or spritsail, they do have their uses.

Modern Bermudian sails work well upwind and on close reaches. However, if the wind is aft of the beam, for a satisfactory performance, you need to hoist special sails. Large balloon-like spinnakers create a lot of drag and are used whenever the course is 120 degrees or further off the wind. Blister sails or cruising chutes and the now fashionable gennakers can be used on all downwind courses and even on extremely shy reaches. Again, we shall take a

closer look at the trim of downwind sails like these at a later stage.

Two or more sails?

Most of us are used to boats with one mast and essentially two sails: a mainsail and a headsail. It's a common arrangement but one which over the years has spawned a number of complicated theories about the way the sails themselves interact not just with the wind but also with each other. To start with the practical considerations, on a sloop, the mainsail would normally be set first when you get underway. Sailing under mainsail alone, the boat will gather momentum and remain manoeuvrable. On a lot of boats, you might even be able to beat to windward a little under just the main alone. But the real potential of the

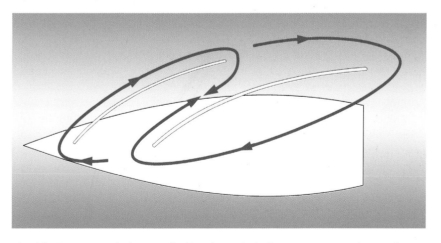

▲ *What's wrong with the so called 'jet theory'? Well, as you can see here, when the 'jet' circulates round the main and jib, it runs in opposite directions.*

boat will only unfold once you set a headsail as well. With both sails hoisted, the boat will not only be faster, but will also sail closer to the wind. This applies equally to sloops with a fractional rig, which have smaller headsails and a larger main. This dramatic increase in performance is not only the result of increased sail area; there are more complex reasons.

People often talk about the popular 'jet theory' when trying to explain this particular phenomenon. It maintains that in the gap between foresail and mainsail, the flow gets speeded up, as it would in a jet. Accordingly, the flow across the lee of the mainsail is increased which in turn produces more lift.

The theory itself was originally formulated by the physician Ludwig Prantl in the 1930s. What he said was that air flows through the small gap between the wings at high speed and thus provides the tired air particles with new energy thus helping them resist the rise in pressure and flow along to the end of the wing, rather than tearing off prematurely.

However, the air inside a jet is accelerated more, if the diameter of the jet is reduced. If Prantl had been right, it would mean you could increase the flow across the mainsail by decreasing the gap between the headsail and main, thereby increasing lift and drive.

This is easy to test in practice. Simply sail close to the wind, then sheet in both sails until you get them just right. Then decrease the gap between jib and main by sheeting in the foresail. Rather than proving the 'jet theory', the exact opposite occurs. The boat doesn't sail faster, but instead slows down. The main loses its shape behind the luff and bellies in towards the windward side. The boat will accelerate again only when you sheet in the main until the windward belly disappears and the gap between the sails increases once more. That, by the way, is how a boat should be trimmed for upwind work. First determine the optimum shape of the foresail (angle to the wind, twist and profile) then sheet in the main until it is full of wind from luff to leech.

The circulation works on both sails. In the gap between main and jib, the flow circulates in opposite directions. The air gets jammed and the flow is reduced. The flow across the forward part of the mainsail is slower and the stagnation point, where the flow gets divided between the windward and leeward sides, moves further forward until it's in front of the mast. This softer approach of the flow allows the sail to be angled more without the flow tearing off along the lee side. At the same time, the circulation around the foresail is increased and the flow across its lee side is substantially intensified.

So, in fact far from increasing the flow across the mainsail, the jet strengthens the circulation around the foresail, which in turn becomes the more effective sail in the system. However, the correct trim of the mainsail has an important bearing on the effectiveness of the foresail.

So if two sails work better than one, why not increase the overall performance of a rig by adding even more sails?

Indeed, many sails increase the amount of lift when sailing upwind. In the pioneering days of aeroplanes, aviation engineers harnessed this effect by building not only double-winged but even triple and multiple winged aircraft. They however also quickly realised that multi-winged planes not only created a lot of lift, but also a lot of drag. So when aircraft became more powerful, which, in practice, meant they flew quicker and higher, single-wing planes with optimised wing profiles proved the best solution.

The same principle applies to any sailing boat. Multiple sails create more lift, but also more drag. Consequently, one of the most effective modern rigs is the Bermudian sloop.

And now for the science bit

While aviation, even in its earliest days, benefited from scientific research, sailing long remained more of an art. Until late in the 20th century, yachts were built using traditions handed down from generation to generation. In the same way, sail-making was a handicraft and a skill, with no firm scientific base.

All that changed when American and, later, European sailors discovered that money could be made from racing. With that realisation, investment into scientific research suddenly made sense. The aim of the research was simple: to find ways of building fast yachts that could win races inside the framework of the relevant racing and rating rules.

For a long time, more or less simple measurement rules like the 'Builders Old Measurement' (BOM) or the 'International Offshore Rule' (IOR) governed the way yachts

▲ *Traditionally, the physical characteristics of a yacht were studied in test tanks like this.*

developed. However, they only considered the geometric size of a boat. In 1985, the 'International Measurement System' (IMS) replaced the old IOR. Today, IMS is the primary system used to make comparisons between the potential speeds of different yachts. The core of the IMS system is revolutionary. It no longer uses simple geometric sizes as the basis for a rating or the difference between winning or losing, but instead looks at the potential speed of a boat and the time it takes to complete a course.

Velocity Prediction Programme (VPP)

The theoretical maximum speed of a yacht is calculated with a 'Velocity Prediction Programme' (VPP). The parameters consist of a great number of measurements taken from the hull, rig and sails. The basis for the accuracy of the VPP is in-depth knowledge of hydrodynamics and aerodynamics. Traditionally, designers would study such things by tank testing models. But with ever increasing computer capacity, numeric ways of conducting research are becoming more and more important.

Even so, the VPP still only delivers a very rough interpretation of reality. A high capacity computer might be able to make a more accurate Navier Stokes calculation, where the pressures and the distribution of forces as well as speeds around hull,

keel, and rudder could be specified but this complicated non-linear system with around three million unknown factors would leave even a large computer sweating away for two or three days. To make matters worse, the calculation would then have to be repeated maybe ten times or more to take into account all the different courses and sail combinations. Yacht designers, whose computer work stations are considerably smaller, would never able to do it.

To increase the accuracy of the VPP, it's necessary to compare the calculated data with reality; in other words, with data that stems from a real yacht sailing under real conditions. The hydrodynamic and aerodynamic forces measured here can then be compared with the results from tank testing and computer programs. The overall result emerges as a database which helps to verify and modify the existing VPP.

That's the theoretical basis. To transfer all this into practice has proved rather difficult. A sailing yacht is a complex thing that sails on the border of two different mediums, water and air. If a yacht sails fast and well, her designer will be happy. But deep down, even he might not really know precisely why the boat performs so efficiently. Is it down to the fact that the hull is well designed and only creates minimal of resistance? Or is the rig aerodynamically effective and delivers maximum lift? Or have both the hydrodynamic and aerodynamic forces been optimised?

▲ *It's impossible to study the interaction between hydrodynamic and aerodynamic forces in tank or wind tunnel testing.*

This kind of guess-work is even worse if the yacht fails to live up to expectations. Should the hull be modified to produce less resistance? Or is it the rig that needs to be changed? Or maybe both?

Using wind tunnels and test tanks you can examine the rig and the hull, but only individually, not as the complete and interacting system it is in reality. But such interactions are extremely important. The rig not only delivers forward momentum, but also side forces which need to be compensated by the keel and rudder. The movements of a boat in seas and in gusts aren't at all predictable but do highly influence the forces at work in both the rig and the underwater hull shape.

Sail-dynanometers

One solution to these problems might be found in a new measuring instrument developed by scientists at the Technical University of Berlin. This is the so-called sail-dynanometer, an instrument designed to measure the forces at work on a yacht under sail. In fact, this dynanometer is nothing more than a sailing boat, in this case a Dehler 33. To put it another way, it's a scientific research ship or even a ship inside a ship. The outer boat is the normal hull, keel and rudder. Inside, a framework carries the rig with all the standing and running rigging, as well as the winches and relevant fittings. The standing and running rigging are led through fairleads on deck. The inner and the outer boats are only connected to each other by six measuring points. The inner boat, which carries the rigging, is little more than a scale with six components, which can measure the aerodynamic forces and components in all six aspects. It's stiff enough to be able to absorb the stresses of a rig set up as tight as it would be on a racing yacht. The forces acting on the stays and shrouds are also measured.

Similar models have already been constructed in the USA (Milgram, 1993) and in Japan (Masuyama and Fukasawa, 1997). But the central focus of both the American and the Japanese research was aerodynamic forces while hydrodynamic parameters like leeway, angle of heel and boat speed were either ignored or only partially considered.

On the Berlin sail-dynamometer, speed and leeway are measured by a 'laser-log'. This measures the speed of particles drifting past the hull outside and in that way also measures the true speed through the water, not the speed at the border between hull and water where friction would again cause a slight difference. Apart from the laser-log, there's also a built-in log, a towing log and a differential GPS. A fibre-optical system as used in aeroplanes

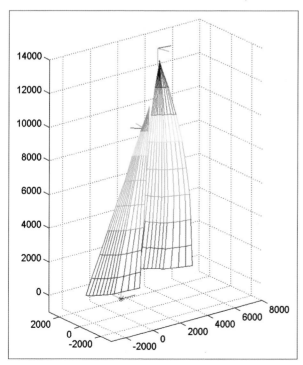

◀ This photographic-geometric measurement system allows Berlin scientists to measure the three-dimensional geometry of the mainsail and the genoa.

records the position of the boat in relation to the three dimensions; forces at the rudder stock are also recorded.

If the aerodynamic and the hydro-dynamic forces are equal, the yacht sails along at a steady speed. The sail-dynanometer measures the driving forces, the resistance forces and the side forces on every course to the wind. Even trim forces are registered.

A measuring device such as the sail-dynanometer provides designers with new knowledge to improve and refine fundamental concepts. One of the main criteria for the performance of a yacht was always speed and efficiency. This also applies to cruising boats. The ability to sail fast and as close to the wind as possible are equally desirable here, because it means shorter passage times and hence, wider horizons. And a good sailing performance is also a safety factor in heavy weather.

The development of yachts' keels, for instance, or the impact of waves on performance can now be improved and enhanced with the help of the sail-dynanometer. And even although the device only exists on one type of boat, the Dehler 33, the scientific data gained here can be applied to other boats too.

▲ The data of the sail's geometry created by the computer is overlaid with the photos of the actual sail shapes.

Scientists at the Technical University in Berlin have undertaken a great number of practical test sails both in the waters around Berlin and in the Baltic. They've even developed an optical measurement system to control the geometry of the sails. During sea-trials, digital cameras on deck and up the mast continuously take pictures of the sails on different points of sailing. In order to be able to compare the photos, the sails have a raster of measurement points in them.

A so-called 'flying shape' of the sails is created from photographic data and sail-geometry calculated by the computer. This is then co-ordinated with the aerodynamic forces for further analysis of the sails.

Using these measurement systems, the developers of the sail-dynamometer have, amongst other things, disproved the long-held belief that aerodynamic forces act in the sail area's centre of effort. Sail trim influences the position of various pressure points. Sailing upwind, for instance, the sail opens up in the upper area and allows the centre of effort to slip lower. This reduces heel. In this way, the effect of applying the correct sail trim as an effective technique for coping with strong winds can be scientifically proved. By trimming the sails properly, you can keep full sail longer and only need to reef later on.

▶ *Along with the standard keel, a number of new, short-draft variants were also tested.*

The results of the keel measurements are also interesting. Short keels with little draft are only inferior to deeper draft keels in higher windspeeds. In light airs, because of their smaller wetted surface area, they actually offer positive advantages both upwind and downwind.

Furthermore, the Berlin scientists were able to prove that winglets do indeed improve the performance of

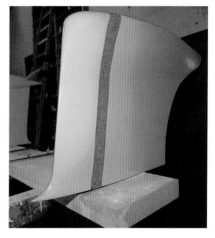

short draft keels. They enhance the aspect ratio of the keel and thus also its ability to deliver hydrodynamic lift. But if the winglets are positioned too far forward along the keel, resistance increases more than lift. The best position is about half way along the bottom of the keel. And finally: winglets only improve performance upwind. When sailing on a reach or downwind, they simply act as brakes.

While the Berlin sail-dynanometer project has ceased operating for the time being, it has however shown quite clearly how data can be obtained under realistic practical conditions which could be used to optimise the design of new boats. We can only hope that the financial backing needed for such projects will also be available in the future and that the designers will make the most of all the hard won data.

Types of rig

On most of the modern production boats around today, the sloop rig is more or less standard. It consists of a main mast supported by stays and shrouds with a (usually) unboomed headsail (jib or genoa) set on a forestay. A groove at the after edge of the mast takes the luff of the mainsail. The foot of the mainsail normally runs inside another groove in the main boom. The boom itself is fastened to the mast with a versatile gooseneck fitting that allows it to be moved in any direction. When hoisted, the head of the unreefed mainsail sits just below the top of the mast.

These days, thanks to roller furling systems, single-line reefing, halyards led aft to the cockpit (not to mention self-tailing winches and modern synthetic sails which owe their performance to aerodynamic efficiency rather than sheer size), it's perfectly possible for a fairly small crew to handle even a big sloop's relatively large sails.

It wasn't always so. Not that long ago, before modern technology intervened on large boats, the total area had to be divided into several smaller and more manageable sails to make handling easier.

Ketches, schooners and cutters

Ketch rigs usually consist of a headsail, a mainsail which would be smaller than a sloop's, and a mizzen set on a second or mizzen mast abaft the main mast. Depending on the course sailed, the sails can easily be adjusted if the wind increases. The mainsail can be taken down altogether and the boat sailed under jib and mizzen alone. Alternatively, the mizzen can be dropped and the yacht sailed under main and jib alone.

A slightly older version of this particular two-masted rig is the yawl. In this format, the mizzen mast is fairly short and the mizzen sail very small, which reduces its effectiveness so its chief function is to help when manoeuvring under sail. In the old days, it was once generally accepted that the mizzen on a yawl was stepped on a line abaft the rudder post but this definition has fallen out of favour. Now, it's often assumed, more simply, that a yawl's mizzen is smaller than that of a ketch and, as a rough rule of thumb, would be between a quarter and a third of the size of the

▶ *Traditional fishing vessels often adopted the ketch rig because the large sail area remained manageable by a small crew.*

mainsail, while the mizzen on a ketch would be at least 50 per cent.

Schooners also have two masts. In this case, the shorter mast would be in front or forward of the taller mainmast and is called a schooner mast. There's no mizzen. A jib is set on the forestay of the schooner mast,

► *Many blue water cruising yachts prefer the cutter rig.*

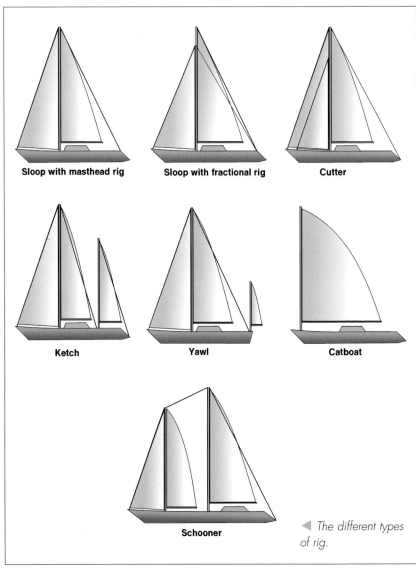

Sloop with masthead rig   Sloop with fractional rig   Cutter

Ketch   Yawl   Catboat

Schooner

◀ *The different types of rig.*

while, in lighter airs, another sail, like a smaller main or staysail might be set between the two masts.

Such split sail plans are a useful way of reducing the size of the respective sails to make them easier to handle. As to their aerodynamic efficiency, however, none of these types of rig are as good as the sloop. Modern boats are very seldom rigged as ketches, schooners or yawls. Having said that, many blue-water sailors prefer a cutter rig because, in contrast to the sloop, it reduces the size of an otherwise substantial genoa into two smaller headsails. Unlike the standard sloop, a cutter can set a fairly large yankee jib, with a high-cut foot and clew, on the jibstay, with a conventional staysail set as a second headsail on the forestay. This would only reach about three quarters of the way up the mast. Often, but not always, the mast might also be supported at this point by running backstays. If the wind freshens, all you would have to do is reduce or drop the jib and carry on under main and staysail alone. However, in the process, the sail-plan's centre of effort would move aft and the yacht might begin to carry excessive weather helm.

Another interesting rig is the cat-rig which is more popular in North America than it is in Europe. Here, there's usually only one sail and one mast, often un-stayed, placed right up in the bow of the boat. The foot of the sail may either have a conventional boom, but more often is set loose-footed in a wishbone boom. A rig like this is fairly easy to handle on all points, since there's only one sail to worry about. Larger catboats have two masts and two sails, again in an effort to keep the respective sail areas manageable. The trim of cat-sails can be difficult, because the unstayed mast and, consequently, the twist and profile of the sail is less easy to control. Because of that, many catboats are not as close-winded as well trimmed sloops.

Sloop rigs can be further broken down into two distinct types: masthead and fractional. In a masthead rig, both the forestay and backstay begin or end at the top of the mast. This type of rig allows the largest possible headsail area when defined by the height of the mast above decks, the length of the forestay and the distance between the foot of the forestay and the foot of the mast. A fractional rig's headsail is slightly smaller because the forestay terminates a fraction of the way down from the top of the mast.

Masthead rig

A masthead rig has several advantages. The headsail, the more effective sail, has a large area and overlaps the main which, in contrast, normally has a fairly short foot and a smaller area. The main strength of the masthead rig is its aerodynamic efficiency and the way it simplifies handling. The mast is supported by a forestay and a backstay as well as shrouds, which are fitted over a pair of spreaders, and end right up at the top of the mast. Lower shrouds further stabilise the mast just below the spreaders. Since the forestay and backstay are both attached to the top of the mast, it's easy to tension the forestay by pulling in the backstay. A tight forestay is important of course because it reduces the curve of the luff and is particularly important when

sailing upwind because it encourages a more efficient profile. A masthead rig is easy to set up. The mast is relatively stable because it's not designed to be bent while underway. Once it's stepped properly and the rigging is adjusted so the mast is straight, you can forget all about tuning it. Cruising sailors find this extremely attractive.

But this is also one of the main drawbacks. Because the mast remains straight, it's impossible to adjust the backstay and change the profile of the main. So, unlike a fractional rig, as there's no way of flattening the profile of the mainsail by bending the mast, it means earlier reefing.

Since the foresail is the larger sail, it makes sense to reduce it first when the wind freshens up. This runs counter to the claim that the masthead rig is easy to handle because, for maximum efficiency in a wide variety of different conditions, you need lots of different headsails. Each wind strength requires its own particular sail. This, in turn, means a considerable amount of potentially hazardous sail handling on the foredeck while underway. Changing a large genoa down to a smaller jib on a wet and heaving deck can also be extremely exhausting especially when sailing short-handed.

◀ *A masthead rig is easy to handle and boasts good aerodynamic properties.*

In mitigation, modern furling genoas which can be rolled in or out at the tug of a string and adjusted in size according to prevailing conditions, have been widely adopted. Even so, and despite all the progress that sailmakers have made trying to improve the design of roller furling sails, a partly rolled genoa will never set as efficiently as a smaller well cut sail. But more about that later.

Fractional rig

The widest used and most popular fractional rig is the 7/8 rig where the forestay terminates roughly 7/8 of the way up the mast. More recently cruising boat designers have sometimes favoured 9/10 rigs which means you can set larger headsails and still retain the flexibility of a tuneable fractional rig. Other boats, like the classic Folkboat for example, have a 3/4 rig.

Because the forestay and backstay are fixed to the mast at different heights, the resulting leverage makes it easy to bend the mast fore-and-aft simply by tightening the backstay. As we've already seen, in the chapter about sail profiles, altering the curve of the mast is an extremely effective method of changing the shape of the main.

Tightening the backstay puts a curve in the mast and makes the top section move back but, further down, near the forestay attachment it arcs forward, so the forestay slackens.

▲ *The mainsail of a fractional rig can be very accurately trimmed.*

▲ *Jumper struts support the top section of the mast and transmit tension from the backstay directly to the forestay.*

Upwind, the profile of the jib will inevitably become baggy and the luff will sag to leeward making it difficult to sail as close to the wind as before. Because of that, the forestay needs some kind of counterbalancing support of its own. The simplest solution is to fit jumper struts at the point where the forestay is attached to the mast. Their job is to transmit the pull of the backstay to the forestay and, and that way, provide additional tension.

Running backstays

Another way of achieving the same end is to fit running backstays – fitted to the mast at the same height as the forestay and led diagonally down and back. Sailing upwind, the running backstay on the boat's windward side is tightened hard so it not only supports the forestay but tensions it. The main backstay is now only used to control the curve of the mast to fine tune the profile of the mainsail. The shrouds only support the mast laterally or athwartships. A second running backstay, might be used as a fine tuning device, and connected to the main runners but ending about half way between the foot of the mast and the permanent backstay.

Beating to windward, you adjust the running backstays on every tack. The old windward runner is released and the old leeward runner, tensioned accordingly. When running downwind or on a broad reach, the windward running backstay would be applied to support the mast at the height of the forestay. If during a gybe, for example, the runners were both loosened while the backstay was still tight, the mast might break above the spreaders.

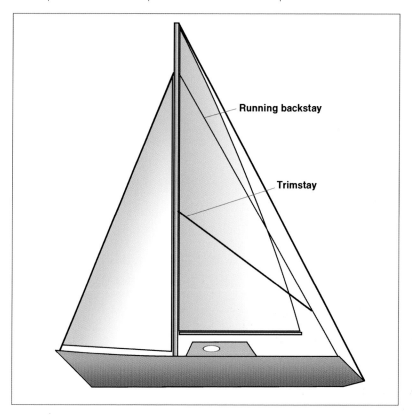

▲ *The running backstay is used to tension the forestay when the mast has been bent by the backstay. The trimstay fine-tunes the curve of the mast.*

Angled spreaders

When used properly, running backstays are highly efficient devices for trimming the mast and sails. However, many cruising sailors find them unsuitable simply because they need almost constant attention. Designers have acknowledged the problem and to that end often eliminate running backstays on fractional rigs by simply angling the spreaders back. Since that encourages the upper shrouds to pull slightly aft, they also support the mast in that direction and at the same time serve to tighten the forestay. The lower shrouds are also set slightly aft and support the mast in a fore-and-aft direction as well as athwartships.

However, it's harder to control the profile of the mainsail so accurately on a fractional rig with angled spreaders than with running backstays. Even with angled spreaders, the tension on the forestay decreases with increasing mast bend. A rig like this has to be set up really tight in the first place to achieve good results when sailing upwind.

In a fractional rig, the headsail is always smaller than the main. That's the reason for its renewed popularity, although for many years, it seemed to have been completely displaced by the masthead rig. Additionally, the IOR (International Offshore Rule) favoured smaller headsails. The area of the headsail counted for 150 per cent when calculating the overall rating of the boat, whereas the area of the main was only rated at 100 per cent.

So, in practice, if the area of the headsail was reduced by a single square metre, the area of the main could be increased by 1.5 square metres without altering the overall rating.

The mainsail is the fractional rig's primary driving force. Consequently, if the wind increases, you can carry on longer with the same headsail, which is already smaller than the main, and instead begin reducing the sail area by flattening or reefing the mainsail. In that way, compared to a boat with masthead rig, the number of sails you have to carry on board is greatly reduced; so is the amount of sail handling work on the foredeck.

On boats with fractional rigs, the mast is placed relatively far forward. That's an advantage when reaching, because a mast in this position reduces any tendency for the boat to yaw away from its course. It also makes it easier to steer. Upwind however, you must control the profile of the main with considerable care. Otherwise, the sail plan's centre of effort will move too far forward and might result in lee helm.

Some unusual rigs

The cockpit rig

Rainer Wieland began sailing when he was 35, first with a Laser dinghy, then with larger, offshore charteryachts. He soon wanted to know exactly how a sailing boat worked and studied everything about aerodynamics and hydrodynamics. He then bought his own boat, but because his wife was less enthusiastic about being on the water, he wanted to be able to sail it single-handed. He decided therefore that it had to have a simple but effective rig: a cutter, but one that he could easily handle by himself.

There was nothing suitable available so he channelled his energies into developing ideas of his own. What he ended up with was the cockpit rig in which the mast is located aft in the cockpit and is attached to a jib stay, a forestay, upper and lower shrouds (which are angled a long way back) and a backstay. A fully battened self-tacking staysail set on the forestay is, in effect, like the mainsail on a conventional rig. The sheet for this sail is led to a traveller forward of the mast.

The staysail is set on the stay further forward, and the mast also has a tiny sail with a very rounded leech, which is set flying without a boom. Wieland reckons that with its large areas, this rig should be reasonably efficient on all points, and because the mast is positioned in the cockpit, it's extremely easy to handle.

Wieland tried his rig on the hull of his own boat. He finished the interior of the boat himself and asked a yacht designer to calculate the dimensions of the rig for him. But the designer refused. After looking at Wieland's plans, he thought the rig would never work. Wieland however wasn't discouraged and instead had a mast built. It was probably a bit too heavy

but there was no doubting its strength. Once the sails had been made, Wieland set off on his first trial sail. His idea worked!

I had the chance to sail his boat for myself in light winds on Lake Constance. The handling was really

▲ *The big advantage of the cockpit rig is a good upwind performance combined with easy handling.*

easy and the sails were set in a moment. Although the wind hardly caused a ripple on the water, the boat sailed at five knots upwind and a bit faster on a beam reach. Downwind, however, the boat was much slower. It would be necessary to use two booms or poles to get both staysails working effectively with the wind aft. And the tiny 'mainsail' had little if any effect, despite its good aerodynamic shape. In flat water, the boat tacked through 80 degrees, which equals 40 degrees to the wind. The foot of the genoa is quite short so the clew can pass the forestay easily when tacking.

The directional stability of the boat is remarkable. Once the sails were trimmed, the boat sailed happily along with a lashed tiller. Needless to say, Rainer Wieland is highly satisfied with his cockpit rig. The big advantages are the easy handling, the absence of a main boom, and the good upwind characteristics. However, to qualify as a real alternative for cruising boats, it would be necessary to improve the performance downwind and on a reach.

The trapeze rig

The trapeze rig, developed by the designer Horst Glacer back in 1981 first saw the light of day as a theoretical concept only, details of which were published in the yachting magazine *Yacht*. What Glacer wanted to do was to solve the cruising skipper's old dilemma: how to combine a decent sail area to keep a boat

moving even in light airs, with the ability to reef quickly and efficiently with the minimum of manpower. He looked at traditional two-masted solutions but discarded them on grounds of inefficiency. As we've already seen, the aerodynamic efficiency of a mizzen on a ketch, for example, is poor and upwind, the sail contributes more drag than lift. Not only that, the sail's centre of effort wanders along the boat's centre line as soon as the mizzen is taken down which encourages yawing. Finally, a ketch rig is expensive, because you will need a second mast with all attendant rigging and fittings.

So, instead, Horst Glacer went down a totally different route. The result was something he called the trapeze rig. He cut down the total area of the main by dividing it up into a staysail and a sail rather like a fisherman; indeed, the whole concept is similar in some ways to the wishbone rig. The luff of the fisherman sail sits in the mast groove. Thanks to the ingenious design of the backstay, Glacer needs neither a second mast nor a wishbone for the second sail. Instead, he fitted twin backstays pushed apart by a bar. From the middle of the bar, a profiled stay runs down to the foot of the mast. This carries a furling system on which the staysail is set.

The backstay bar also has a traveller, on which the sheet of the fisherman is set. The lead is located far up in the rigging so it's possible to trim the profile and the angle of the

▲ The trapeze rig driving a heavy displacement yacht along at high speed even in a light breeze.

▲ *A bar pushes the twin backstays apart. There's a traveller mounted at this point for the sheet of the fisherman; the head of the roller stay for the staysail is also fitted here.*

fisherman almost to perfection. Only on a reach does the short traveller become ineffective, at which point the clew of the sail begins to collapse to windward.

The fisherman is the mainsail in this configuration. It's used purely as a light-weather sail. Since it's very effective aerodynamically, it drives the boat well even in light airs. As soon as the wind reaches around force 3, you take the fisherman down. It's led down the mast groove into a sail bag and zipped up tight. In this way, it's securely stowed but can easily be set again at any time.

The centre of effort of the sails slips vertically downwards when the fisherman is taken in, so no yawing tendencies are induced. It also reduces the heeling factor. After reefing in this way, the boat will sail much better than a ketch without a mizzen. If the wind increases further, all the reefing can be done from the safety of the cockpit.

First the genoa and then the staysail would be reefed. Because the staysail is set flying, there's no boom.

Taking down the sails when entering harbour is also very easy. The fisherman disappears into its bag; the other sails are furled away.

The trapeze rig however has one structural problem. Because the staysail is only fixed at the foot of the mast and in the rigging, there's a real danger that the rig will begin to vibrate and swing until the boat is no longer under control. Glacer found a solution by introducing further support for the spreader bar between the backstays by adding two preventers, – rather like running backstays – and two further stays that cross each other and run down to the stern. However, the standing rigging on a yacht with trapeze rig must be set up as hard as the hull structure will allow.

Every sloop rig could be converted into a trapeze rig fairly easily and without too much expense. You could still use the original mast for instance, and so could the foresail. The only additions would be the twin

▲ *The sail bag for the fisherman is fixed to the mast.*

▲ *While the fisherman can be neatly trimmed upwind, the clew tends to collapse to windward on a run.*

backstays complete with spreader bar and the two new sails behind the mast. The first boat to be rigged like this was a production 36 footer. This design displaces 8.5 tons and has a waterline length of 9 metres. In 1995, I sailed her in the Mediterranean and was positively surprised by her performance. In a very light breeze, she sailed upwind at 50 degrees and made about 5 knots. Her directional stability was remarkable; once the sails had been trimmed she would sail a straight course with the helm lashed. In a force 3, the boat reached its hull speed of 7.3 knots. However, it heeled over quite a bit and luffed up in the gusts. Once we'd taken down

the fisherman, the boat was a lot steadier but she still sailed fairly fast.

On a reach, however, for reasons already explained, it was impossible to trim the fisherman correctly. Also, in fresh winds, the stay of the staysail sagged off to leeward quite a bit which made it impossible to trim the sail flat any further. If you reduce the sail area by furling the staysail and genoa, you get the same old problems you always run into with roller furling sails, but in this case the drawbacks are multiplied by two.

Despite all that, the trapeze rig seems to be an interesting alternative to the conventional sloop rig, although it's yet to win a significant share of the market.

Sailcloth

The stiffer a sailcloth is, and the less tendency it has to stretch, the better its profile can be controlled. That's easy to understand: a cloth that stretches under pressure will become baggy in strong winds, which is the exact opposite of what we normally want. Moreover, the position of the deepest part of the profile is entirely dependent on the tensile characteristics of the cloth and completely beyond our control.

The importance of stiff and stable cloths was dramatically demonstrated in the mid 19th century. In those days, sails were made from natural fibres, normally flax. The sailing elite assembled in 1851 for their annual race around the Isle of Wight. As a guest and a crass outsider, the American schooner *America* also took part in this race. None of the members of the British sailing establishment thought she had the slightest chance of winning. So everyone was deeply shocked when it transpired that the schooner was much faster and more close-winded upwind and eventually won the race. The secret of her success lay in the sails. The Americans were using cotton instead of flax, which was much more tightly woven and far less

prone to stretch than traditional alternatives. The schooner's sails could therefore be trimmed flatter than those of the competition, and as a result, she was faster upwind.

Synthetic cloth

Today's sailcloths are made from synthetic fibres. Most cruising boats use cloths made from polyester fibres marketed under the trade name Dacron (DuPont) or Terylene (ICI). The polyamide fibre Nylon is also made by DuPont. Nylon stretches a great deal more than Dacron but is considerably lighter in weight and for that reason is used for downwind sails like spinnakers etc.

Laminated fibres have been produced since the mid 1970s. Mylar was particularly popular for a time. It was basically a thin sheet made of polyester resin. However, spinnakers made from pure Mylar film for the America's Cup in 1964 weren't a great success and, since then, Mylar has only been used as a laminate in conjunction with polyester cloths.

Kevlar, the aramid fibre, has been acclaimed as a truly revolutionary material. It's very strong and at the same time extremely light. On the downside, Kevlar is affected by the sun's UV rays and the fibres break easily when they get creased into folds. Kevlar sails have to be stowed under sun awnings when not in use and should never be allowed to flap excessively when set. Today, aramid is interwoven with polyester fibres and the resulting cloth laminated with Mylar.

Spectra cloths are also highly resistant to stretch. Made from a special polyethylene fibre they too are normally laminated as a cloth with Mylar. This is nearly as strong as Kevlar but even lighter. However, Spectra can be overstretched sooner than Kevlar and will then lose its shape. Dyneema is also made from polyethylene and has similar characteristics to Spectra.

Vectran cloths are nearly as strong as those made of Kevlar and have one distinct advantage: Vectran is less sensitive to folding or even breaking. On the downside, it's even more vulnerable to the sun's UV rays, and costs about 50 per cent more than Kevlar.

Carbon fibre sails are very rare. The cloth is extremely stiff but rather expensive and the fibres are even more easily broken than Kevlar when the sail is folded.

Sail cut

Apart from the material, the method of weaving and the cut of a sail also influence its stability and tendency to stretch. Sailcloth is woven from two fibres: the *warp* and *weft* yarns. The warp yarn is also called the zero-degree yarn because it runs along the length of the cloth; the weft yarn is also called the 90 per cent yarn as it runs across the warp yarn at right angles. If these yarns are woven with different tensions, the cloth's tendency to stretch is reduced in the direction of the tighter yarn.

Sailcloths are often oriented along the warp yarns, which means that there is less stretch in the direction of the warp yarn. Sails are made of several panels of cloth which are stitched together. These panels should be cut in such a way that they are particularly resistant to stretch in the direction of the greatest forces in the sail. The mainsails of cruising yachts are often made from horizontal panels of weft-oriented cloth. The main forces that travel from the clew of the sail to the head are well compensated for here, and the after leech will also keep its shape. In the jib or genoa, the lines of largest stress run from the clew roughly diagonally to the middle of the luff. Headsails are often made from horizontal panels of cloth in which the warp and weft yarns have roughly equal tension and strength

Radial-pattern sails are even more complex. In a tri-radial cut, the panels emanate like rays from the point of the highest stress to the middle of the sail; the panels themselves usually begin at the head, the tack and the

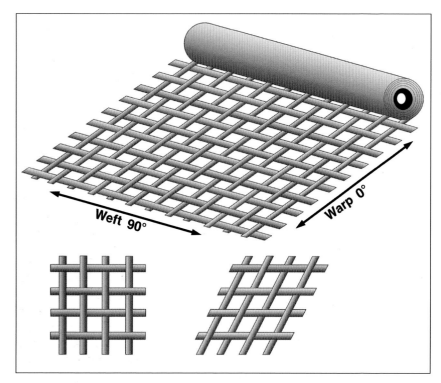

▲ *The structure of sailcloth. Normally, there are no diagonal yarns, so the cloth is sensitive to stretching in that direction. Diagonal stresses in the sail must either be eliminated, or the cloth strengthened, by laminating several layers.*

clew of the sail. In some sails, only the corners are designed in a radial pattern, with the rest made from horizontal panels. The imagination and creativity of the sail-maker is limitless in this respect! However, the more complex the cut of the sail, the more expensive it will probably be. Highly competitive and ambitious racing sailors will have to pay this price, while the average cruising sailor will be more than satisfied with a proven but simple cut and a good quality cloth.

Rig trim

Before we finally look at the practical side of trimming sails, I would like to add one last morsel of theory. Under sail, every boat displays one inherent characteristic: yawing off course. Within certain limits you can reduce this tendency by finding the correct trim of the rig and sails. But first, let's see why the tendency to yaw occurs in the first place.

Yawing

Yawing means that the yacht veers off course by itself, without anyone touching the rudder. If it turns to windward, the boat has *weather helm*, if she falls off to leeward, she carries *lee helm*. These characteristics exist because the yacht is sailing on the edge of two different mediums: water and air. The forces at work below the waterline are different from those acting on the rigging and sails.

To make it simpler, imagine for a moment that all the combined forces above and below the water are concentrated into one single spot. The hydrodynamic forces created by the keel and the rudder act on the lateral centre of effort; the aerodynamic forces act on the sail's centre of effort. These centres of effort are rarely ever located in the same place and are the geometric centres of the individual areas. The centres of effort depend on the distribution of pressures on the respective profiles that create lift and thus alter as the angle of flow or the speed of flow changes. Also, when the boat heels, the centres of effort change.

If all these influences are equal and act along a single line, the boat will be stable and sail at a steady speed and a steady angle of heel on a straight course.

The aerodynamic side-force on the sail plan and the hydrodynamic side-force on the keel both act more or less at right angles to the course, and differ from the centreline by the angle of leeway. If the boat is heeled, it mainly rotates around its centreline. The sail plan's centre of effort moves to leeward; the hydrodynamic centre of effort moves to windward. Since these forces don't act at right angles to the centreline of the boat, but to the course, the aerodynamic centre of effort also moves slightly aft and the hydrodynamic centre of effort moves slightly forward. This in turn creates the turning momentum that encourages the tendency for the

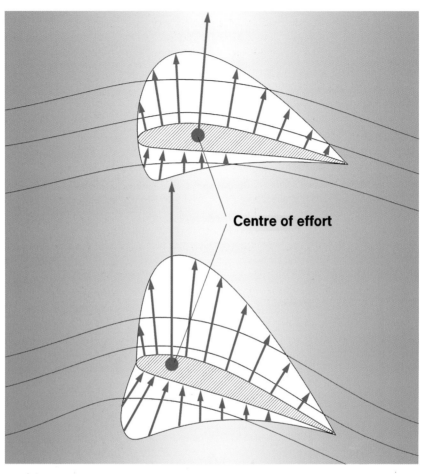

Centre of effort

▲ *The distribution of the pressure along a wing changes with the angle and speed of the flow.*

yacht to turn to windward, which means she carries weather helm. A small amount of weather helm is desirable because it can be corrected by the rudder which creates additional lift to windward. By correcting the course, the rudder will be at a slight angle to the flow and also acts like a small wing. In that way, it helps you to sail the yacht closer to the wind. Moreover, many sailors like the feel of a rudder that carries just a modicum of weather helm which gives them feedback through the tiller and 'something to steer against'. A perfectly balanced boat, on the other hand, would feel dead and lifeless.

If weather helm increases as the boat continues to heel, the course must be corrected by pulling the tiller up further and increasing the angle of the rudder. Form a certain point onwards, drag will be stronger than lift. Instead of sailing closer to the wind, the rudder will only act like a brake. If the angle of heel and the tendency to yaw to windward is too great, at some point the flow will tear off from the rudder. The wake of the boat will begin to bubble and foam, and the boat will shoot up into the wind as the rudder loses its grip. A rudder angle of about five degrees is helpful, anything over that soon becomes counter-productive.

The attitude of the wetted surface of the boat changes constantly and especially with increasing heel. Not only that, the position of the two centres of effort also move in relation to each other. The more the boat heels, the more it develops a tendency to yaw to windward. In practice it's impossible to achieve a stable configuration of the boat at every angle of heel. Normally, boats are designed in such a way that the

▶ *A yacht sailing in a state of stability*

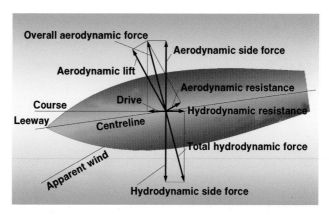

▶ *When the cente of effort of both the sails and the lateral sections move away from each other, a turning momentum is created that encourages the yacht to yaw from its course*

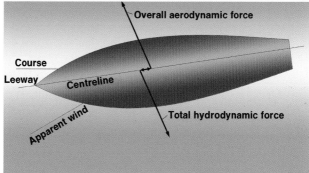

aerodynamic centre of effort is slightly forward of the hydrodynamic centre of effort when the boat is upright. If sailed completely upright, the boat would then carry slight lee helm. When heeled, this would quickly reverse to slight windward helm. How far the two centres of effort should be positioned away from each other depends on the form of the hull and keel as well as the rig. The art of designing a sailing boat also encompasses the challenge of locating the centres of effort for different sail combinations and placing them in precisely the right positions.

As a rule of thumb for a masthead rigged sloop, the hydrodynamic centre of effort should be aft of the aerodynamic centre of effort by about five to nine per cent of the waterline length when the boat is upright.

Finally, let's look at the practical side of sailing. To use all the control lines etc to full effect on a modern yacht, you must first set up the rigging in the right way. Since modern cruising boats are nowadays nearly all sloop-rigged, we shall only look at tuning the sloop rig. However, we must of course differentiate between masthead and fractional rig.

Tuning the masthead rig

As we've already seen, the masthead sloop has established itself as most yachtsmen's rig of choice. Equally clear is the reason for its popularity: it's simple and uncomplicated. That translates into a number of practical advantages: the main one being that it's easy to work with. It's undeniable that It only offers a limited range of sail trim possibilities but the big advantage right from the start is that it's easy to set up and tune.

So, where do you start? First, you should take a look at the rake of the mast. If it's raked towards the stern, the aerodynamic centre of effort will also be further aft. The spar of a masthead-rigged sloop should have a slight rake so the boat carries moderate weather helm when heeled at a modest angle. The boat will then be easy to steer and the slightly angled rudder will increase the amount of hydrodynamic lift, enabling the boat to sail closer to the wind. A mast which is raked slightly aft also makes the boat go faster when sailing upwind; this effect will be even more pronounced in stronger winds.

Precisely how far the mast can be raked aft differs from boat to boat and from rig to rig. The correct amount of rake can only be established by trial and error – but under no circumstances should the mast be raked so far back that the rudder has to be angled more than five degrees to counteract weather helm.

The rake of the mast will alter with the position of the foot of the mast. If it's fixed in one position, as is the case in most cruising boats, it can be adjusted through the length of the forestay. In practice, you loosen the forestay and then tighten the backstay until the forestay is taut again.

The mast of a masthead-rigged boat should not only be slightly raked aft, but also have a slight curve. To achieve the desired result, the forward lower shrouds would be set up tighter than the aft lower shrouds, thus pulling the spar forward by way of the spreaders. The top of the mast will move slightly aft.

When you later hoist the genoa and set the halyard up tight, the top of the mast will be pulled forwards. A mast which is slightly bent when not under any load will be straight when sailing. If the mast is straight when it's not under load, the top might be pulled towards the bows when sailing. The mast will then be bent forward and the after leech of the mainsail will be far too tight. The main will become baggy and the leech will 'close', or curve to windward. As a result, the boat will heel excessively and develop far too much weather helm.

It follows, therefore, that under no circumstances should the mast be set up in such away that it is bent forward when not under any load. The negative effects already mentioned would be even more pronounced.

The mast should always be straight when viewed from directly ahead or astern; there should be no bias to either side. To check, simply look up the mainsail groove from the gooseneck fitting. If the mast is bent to one side, it means the shrouds on that side have been tensioned too much and need to be re-adjusted.

Some sailors have the strange idea that a rig can be set up really tight by

▶ *On many boats, the position of the mast is determined by the designer and can only be stepped in a pre-determined spot. If you want to increase mast rake, you must adjust the length of the forestay on the bottle screw. However, you should remember to adjust both the shrouds and the backstay afterwards.*

tightening the leeward shrouds when sailing upwind, then tacking and tightening the new leeward shrouds, then tacking again and so forth. I've no idea who started the myth but it's a dangerous misconception. In theory, you could carry on with this game until the mast was bent like a banana and the chainplates had been ripped off the boat or something had broken.

The simple fact of the matter is that the leeward shrouds will always be looser than the windward shrouds, no matter how brutally they might be tightened, so this particular technique is completely nonsensical and can only damage the boat, the rig and the fittings. Finally, If the mast is bent sideways in a double S-form, it means the shrouds or stays are too tight and should be slackened off a little.

Tuning the fractional rig

In the chapter about different types of rig, we established that fractional rigs can have either running backstays or spreaders that are angled or swept back aft.

The upper shrouds on a fractional rig with angled spreaders pull the shrouds slightly aft to tighten the forestay; it's vital to get the tension of these upper shrouds just right to get the desired result. On a rig like this, the upper shrouds must be set up as hard as possible. Otherwise the forestay will sag when you're sailing upwind and the foresail's profile will soon become too baggy. It's best to adjust the tension of the upper shrouds while the boat is moored and the mast has no load. You bend the mast backwards by tightening the backstay or, if there's no backstay, use the mainsail halyard or the boom's topping lift to pull the top of the mast backwards. This will reduce the tension on the upper shrouds and make it easier to set them up really tight. Once the upper shrouds have been tightened, you simply release the load at the masthead and the rig will now have exactly the right amount of tension.

Tension on the upper shrouds is also necessary to support the mast in heavy weather when the mainsail is deeply reefed. Once reefed, the sail won't support the upper part of the mast any more. In this state the spar is free to snap or break above the spreaders if the boat crashes heavily in a big sea. Similarly, the lower shrouds that support the mast aft should also have a certain amount of tension. However, if the lower shrouds are tensioned too much, the curve of the mast will be straightened and the possibility of flattening the mainsail will be reduced.

The more the shape the mainsail has, the bendier the mast should be to allow the main to be trimmed for every wind strength. A slight curve of the mast can be pre-set to optimise the air-flow across the mainsail, even when the backstay is completely slack in light airs.

If the fractional rig in question has running backstays and straight spreaders, the shrouds will only serve to hold the mast straight in a sideways direction. The forestay will be tensioned with the running backstays and the curve of the mast controlled by the trimstays and the backstay.

The even tension of the shrouds can be controlled in exactly the same way as with the masthead rig: by looking up the mainsail track. Again, the shrouds should never be so tight that the mast is unable to bend sideways. If it does, loosen the shrouds just far enough to allow the spar to straighten up again.

Sail trim in practice

Remember the theory? As we said at the start, to trim a sail correctly on a specific course means adjusting its profile and angle to the wind in such a way that the relationship between lift and drag is the best it can possibly be. But that's only half the story. At the same time, the forces above and below the waterline should also be as balanced as possible to avoid any excessive tendency to yaw. The precise relationship of lift and drag, which is called the *gliding factor* can be different, depending on the prevailing conditions.

- When sailing upwind, we want as much lift and as little drag as possible. We want the boat to get sucked along to windward as effortlessly as possible. By the same token, The freer the wind is in relation to the course being steered, the more drag can be allowed along with the lift. On the other hand, when sailing down-wind, everything is different. Lift has no bearing any more and you want the sails to create the maximum aerodynamic resistance to drive the boat along as fast as possible.

- As we've seen, when sailing upwind in light airs, you need the maximum lift to keep the boat going. To achieve that, what you want from the sail is a deep, powerful profile even though that will inevitably increase the total amount of aerodynamic drag. In other words, it's a trade-off. This is especially relevant if an awkward swell further slows the boat down. At the same time, the angle of the sail should be as large as possible to create maximum lift, even if that means accepting the penalty of increased drag.

- If the wind is fresher, you get more aerodynamic drag which in turn means a greater angle of heel which does you no good at all. In a situation like that, therefore, it's advisable to make sure the sail's profile is as flat as possible. That's the best way to reduce drag and heel. Otherwise the boat will develop excessive weather helm which would only slow it down. Also the angle to the wind should be kept small. At this point, it's now more important to find a better or more practical relationship between lift and drag rather than trying to achieve maximum lift.

- In light airs, the speed of the true wind changes with height to a considerably greater extent than it does in fresh breezes. In light winds, the twist of the sail should be extremely pronounced to take advantage of the situation and the leech should be open.
- A pronounced twist can also be helpful in stronger breezes. If you adjust everything so the sail doesn't develop the same curve in its upper part, there's less lift and the centre of effort of the sail moves downwards. That in turn reduces the boat's angle of heel which only slows you down.

Trimming the mainsail

High aspect ratio
A tall narrow triangular sail – in other words, one which has a high aspect ratio – is the most efficient form when sailing upwind. Here we are looking at the ratio of luff length (leading edge) to the foot. For an upwind sail, the leading edge should be as long as possible, while the foot can be extremely short. It's easy to see why because the longer the leading edge, the more lift is created. And the shorter the foot, the less induced resistance there is because of the compensation of pressure that flows around the base of the sail (or wing). If you took things to extremes, the best solution for upwind sailing would be a stiff wing profile like the wing mast on Dennis Conner's America's Cup catamaran *Stars and Stripes*. Downwind, however, the ratio can be less, with a shorter luff and a longer foot. The induced resistance created by the pressure compensation around the foot will now work in the direction of the course sailed.

A yacht's sail is always a compromise between two extremes, between good upwind characteristics and a good downwind characteristics. The length of the luff is determined by the boat's designer, so there's little you can do about that. Boats with a masthead rig normally have a higher aspect ratio mainsail than those with a fractional rig. The shorter boom makes it easier to identify.

Leech curve
Having considered the length of the luff and the foot, it's worth looking at the other side of the triangle. The leech of our mainsail should always be as rounded and curved as possible. That's because a rounded shape has more surface area in the upper part. Furthermore, a sail (or wing) with an elliptical trailing edge is aerodynamically more efficient than one with a straight leech. The former will deliver more lift and less drag.

That's all very well, but how does that work out in practice? To prevent the elliptical leech from sagging off to leeward, it needs support and has to be held by horizontal battens, which would normally be inserted into pockets sewn into the sail. These battens should be as light as possible because their function is to support the leech but not to drag the sail downwards. On the other hand, they need to be stiff to maintain the shape of the sail, even in stronger winds.

Battens whose flexibility changes along their length are best. They should be completely stiff at their after end but become increasingly more flexible along their length. The best solution would be to have different sets of battens on board, for all kinds of weather conditions. As the American racing skipper Dennis Conner once said 'No real racing sailor will only use the battens that the sail-maker has provided.'

Some sails go much further and are 'fully battened', which means that the battens go right across the sail

from leech to luff. The leech of a fully battened mainsail can be cut with a very pronounced elliptical shape as long as it stays clear of the backstay. With this arrangement, it means that the profile of a fully battened sail holds its shape even in very light airs. But there's a snag. If the battens are somewhat stiff or under tension, they can remain in the same curved position even after a tack. The sail's profile will then point to windward. In such cases it usually helps to pull the boom to weather then give it a firm shove back to leeward whereupon the battens will flop over to leeward with a loud 'plop'.

The mainsails on many modern cruising boats are only fully battened at the top. The two uppermost battens

▲ *Fully battened mainsails are particularly effective upwind.*

▲ *The sail can easily be stowed on the boom when taken down because the battens keep the sail straight. However, a fully battened mainsail can only be set and taken down with the boat head-to-wind.*

will reach across the sail from leech to luff; the other battens will be shorter.

Advantages of the fully battened main:
- The leech can be more rounded.
- The sail creates less drag upwind.
- The sail's profile remains in shape even in light airs and choppy seas.
- The stresses on the cloth are reduced upwind.
- The sail won't shake like a flag when tacking or gybing.
- The sail lasts longer because it doesn't flap about.
- Differently tensioned battens increase the possibilities of trim.

Disadvantages of the fully battened main:
- A fully battened main can only be set and taken down when the boat is exactly head-to-wind.
- Setting the sail is often not very easy.
- The battens require special fittings – expensive batten cars for instance.
- A fully battened main produces less drive downwind than a conventional sail.
- When rounding up into the wind, the sail often continues to pull for much longer than may be anticipated.

- A fully battened main is considerably more expensive than a conventional main.
- The fully battened main is heavier.
- On a reach, the battens will inevitably chafe on the shrouds.

Tell-tales

The mainsail has an arsenal of trimming controls. The two most obvious ones are the traveller and mainsheet. The traveller regulates the angle to the wind while the mainsheet controls the twist of the sail. In practice, the two are used together to achieve the best angle and shape for different conditions.

But how do you know when you've got it right? Since you can't see the flow of air past the sail, you need some way of making it visible. Only then can you really fine-tune the angle and the twist.

An extremely simple and highly effective method of achieving this is by using small nylon or cotton threads which you can easily cut up yourself and fix to the sail. Such threads are

▲ Left: *Tell-tales positioned along the leech are extremely useful indicators and show exactly how the flow leaves the sail. This particular sail has been trimmed flat for fresh winds but as you can see, the leech is too open in the upper part; consequently the tell-tale points forward.*

Centre: *The traveller has been let out to leeward and the sheet tightened accordingly. The leech has closed slightly and the twist is now about right. The upper batten is roughly parallel to the boom and the upper tell-tale only points forward from time to time.*

Right: *If the sheet is taken in harder, the leech will close up and the twist will be too small. If that happens, the upper tell-tale will point forward all the time.*

called tell-tales. In a laminar stream, they always point aft. If the flow tears off, they point forwards or upwards. In a turbulent flow they generally flutter about restlessly in circles.

Fix three or four of these tell-tales to the leech of your main to show the flow of air in this area. It's important, however, to fix them to the same side of the sail in order to compare them with each other.

Angle and twist

It's amazing how many cruising skippers fail to make the most of their main sheet travellers. In practice, both the traveller and the mainsheet should be adjusted in different ways depending on the particular weather conditions you might encounter. In light airs, and when sailing upwind, the traveller should be on the centre-line of the boat or even slightly to windward, while the sheet would be loose. The end of the boom is then allowed to rise and the tension on the

leech will be reduced. As a consequence, the leech will open and the twist become more pronounced. You should loosen the sheet only until the lower tell-tales flow straight aft and the top tell-tale flops around to the front from time to time. That tells you that the angle is correct, the leech is open, and you have the right amount of twist.

If the sheet is too loose, the twist may become exaggerated. Even the top tell-tale will then stream out aft. If, on the other hand, the sheet is too tight, the leech will close to windward so the flow will be unable to leave the trailing edge of the lower part of the sail in a straight line; the tell-tales will then also point forward at this stage.

If the wind increases, you really need to reduce the twist of the mainsail. To do that, you move the traveller to leeward and haul in the sheet tighter. The angle will remain roughly the same, but the leech will

▶ *On a reach, the twist of the main is controlled by a kicking strap.*

close a bit and the twist will be reduced. The top tell-tale may now point continuously forwards, while the others should again stream aft.

When you bear off on a reach, you will first have to adjust the angle by letting the traveller out even more and then control the twist with the sheet.

The broader the reach, the more the sail can be allowed to twist. This applies in light airs as well as fresh winds.

On a broad reach, the possibilities of the traveller come to a flat stop – literally. Very soon, the traveller car will have reached the outer end of the track which means the only option left is to control the angle with the mainsheet. The shorter the track, the sooner the problem arrives. To prevent the end of the boom from lifting too much, it must now be held down with a kicking strap. This means that you control the angle with the sheet and the twist with the kicker. If you tighten the kicker, the twist will be reduced; if you loosen it, the twist will increase. But in any case, the main should be allowed to twist a bit more on a reach. Some cruising boats don't even have a traveller. It saves money, there's more space in the cockpit and the handling of the boat is considerably simpler. On the other hand, you have less options when it comes to trimming the sail. So it makes sense to install a decent traveller. Even when sailing upwind, twist and angle must be controlled with the sheet and the kicker.

Because the angle of the kicker in relation to the boom isn't always ideal, this operation is more difficult than it is with a traveller.

In strong winds, when sailing upwind or with the wind abeam, it can be almost impossible to set up the kicker hard enough. In these conditions you should haul in the mainsheet as hard as you can, reset the kicking strap so it's not loose, then let out the sheet again until the angle is correct. If the distance along the boom between kicking strap and mast is too short, the kicker will put a lot of strain on the mast. In extreme cases, the mast can break above the gooseneck fitting, or the boom can break at the kicking strap attachment if it's set up too hard in strong winds and big seas.

Profile and shape

One of the main objectives of this book is to encourage skippers to think about every component of their boats as a three-dimensional object. This is particularly important with sails which, as we've seen, unlike simple flat panels, can be persuaded to take up complicated shapes. For that reason we need to be aware of all the possibilities at all times. So, apart from the angle and the twist, the profile of the main must also be right. In light airs and choppy seas, you need a deep, powerful profile with a lot of lift. In strong winds, however, it should be flat to reduce drag and heeling forces, as well as the tendency of the boat to develop weather helm.

▲ Left: *A fractional rig with running backstays and trimstays. The backstay is loose, and the runners and trimstays are slightly tensioned. The forestay is tight and the mast is straight. The mainsail has a deeply-shaped profile.*
Centre: *The windward runner is tight and the backstay has also been tensioned. The mast begins to bend at the top and the main is flatter at this point.*
Right: *The trimstay has now been let out a little so the mast bends evenly over its entire length and now pulls the main flat.*

The best way to control the depth of the sail profile is by mast bend. This works most effectively on boats with fractional rigs, the masts of which can be easily bent with the backstay. In this way, the curve of the mast can be made to match the curve of the mainsail's luff. The sail-maker will have deliberately cut the mainsail in such a way that some additional cloth along the luff will create a deep profile in the sail when the mast is straight. If the mast is bent, however, it will stretch out the additional cloth from the sail and make the profile flatter. If there's a fold that runs from roughly the middle of the luff diagonally across the sail aft to the clew, it means the mast is bent too much. The correct mast curve obviously depends on the cut of the sail and you'll have to find out what it is by experimenting.

Thanks to the curve of the mast, the leech will also open in the upper part of the sail; in other words the twist will increase. In stronger winds, the angle here will now be too small, the sail will fail to develop any lift at this particular point and might even begin to flap. On the other hand, this has the effect of decreasing the pressure in the upper part of the sail, reducing the leverage which contribute to the heeling forces and thus reducing the angle of heel, which is generally particularly welcome in strong winds. Remember that excessive heeling only causes the boat to luff up into the wind which you would have to compensate for with exaggerated movements of the rudder. This would slow you down more than losing a little bit of lift in the upper part of the sail.

The mast on a masthead rig can also be bent by tightening the backstay. Since, in this case, the forestay and backstay are both attached at the same point, the leverage on the fractional rig will be lost. Mast curve can now only be achieved by introducing ram pressures on the mast. Such devices can place a big strain on the boat itself and the ability to bend the mast is strictly limited.

Even when setting the sail, you can already begin to influence the profile. You should set up the halyard so tight that a fold develops in the sail parallel to the mast. This is the extra cloth that you get with a rounded luff, which achieves the shape you want to develop in the first place. This fold should vanish once the sail has been sheeted in and begins to fill with wind. If it doesn't, it means the halyard is too tight and should be slackened off a bit.

The position of the deepest part of the profile also has a huge influence on performance. The best position for it is a point between 35 and 45 per cent of the sail's width behind the luff. If the sail is, say, three metres wide between luff and leech, two-thirds up the mast, the deepest part of the profile here should sit about 1.05 to 1.35 metres behind the luff.

As the wind increases, this deepest part of the profile should be pushed forward to avoid the flow from tearing off too early. Again, the position of the profile can be controlled with the halyard. If it's set up very tight, the profile will wander forwards; if it's loosened, the profile will move aft.

In strong winds, the halyard can only be partially adjusted when sailing and even that requires a great deal of strength. Even when using the halyard winch, this task is not easy. You have to overcome a lot of friction along the full length of the luff and work against the pull of the mainsheet.

It's much easier to use a luff-tensioner, which is also known as a Cunningham. This particular control line, gets its name from Briggs Cunningham, the skipper of the winning America's Cup yacht *Columbia* in 1958. The Cunningham consists of an eye which is sewn into the luff of the main about two hands width above the tack. A line fastened into it leads back to the cockpit and when you pull it tight, the luff is stretched. This has the same effect as tensioning the main halyard but is much easier to accomplish when sailing. If the Cunningham is tensioned, the profile moves forward; if it's let out, the profile slips aft. When setting the sail, the Cunningham must be completely loose.

When you bend the mast to flatten the sail's profile, the deepest part of the shape often moves aft. You can compensate this effect by tightening the Cunningham. However, you should always remember to increase mast bend and Cunningham tension in parallel with each other. In the lower part of the main, the profile is adjusted with the foot tensioner or clew outhaul. However, this should only be loosened in very light airs. In principle, the sail should be as flat as possible just above the boom.

A deep profile increases the difference in pressure between the windward and leeward sides of the sail. The foot and the boom form the base of the profile and the air will flow around and beneath the boom to compensate for the difference in pressure. This flow is undesirable because it increases the induced resistance and also disturbs the flow across the sail. Accordingly, the sail should be flat along the boom to keep the differences in pressure low and avoid induced resistance. The only exception is when sailing in very light airs, when everything must be done to create lift. Also, when sailing dead downwind, the induced resistance works forward and helps the boat along.

Some sails have a special fold along the boom made from very light cloth. It's known as a shelf foot. When you loosen the clew outhaul, this shelf foot will unfold and create a very deep profile along the boom. But once more, this is only useful in extremely light winds and when sailing dead downwind.

The leech of the main normally has a thin leech-line which can be used to tension it. This has only minimal impact on the actual trim of the main, but should be pulled just tight enough to stabilise the leech and stop it from flapping. If you pull it in any tighter, the leech will curl to windward and disturb the flow of air across the sail.

If the sail is very old and the cloth tired and stretched, this effect might be unavoidable when you stabilise the leech with the leech-line. In that case, it might be worth considering having the sail-maker sew on a new leech if the sail is otherwise still in serviceable condition.

On a reach or when running downwind, you can bend the sail battens a bit by tightening the leech-line. This helps to increase the profile of the sail and applies particularly to fully battened sails.

▶ *A tight Cunningham will ease the deepest part of the sail's profile forward.*

Trimming the headsail

There are fewer controls available to help you trim the headsail than there are for the main. However it doesn't follow that fine tuning of the jib or genoa is any less important. Earlier on we saw how the headsail is the more effective of the two sails. Fine adjustment to the main really only serves to provide the headsail with the best possible working conditions. But all would be in vain if the headsail were set like an old pair of trousers. It's necessary to trim the headsail as accurately as you tune the main.

Roller furling

Roller furling headsails are standard on many cruising boats today. They make sail handling so easy that, understandably, most skippers prefer them. Apart from anything else, it means you don't have to hank on and set headsails from the foredeck any more; you can control the size of your headsail with the tug of a string from the comfort and security of the cockpit.

A roller furling foresail is always ready for use; all you have to do is unfurl it. Taking the sail in is equally simple, you just roll it in. It's a far cry from the days when crew were expected to fight thrashing sailcloth, and big unwieldy genoas on a wet and heaving foredeck. And once the sail is furled away, it leaves the foredeck free and uncluttered which makes mooring manoeuvres so much safer and easier. The advantages are obvious but what about the snags?

▲ *Headsail furling gear is standard on most production cruising boats today.*

Modern roller furling systems are fairly reliable and it's unlikely that the mechanism will fail or seize up underway which would make it impossible to roll in the sail. On the other hand, every mechanical piece of equipment has the potential to fail. In rough weather, if the sail suddenly unfolded with a bang or couldn't be furled away, it would present real and serious problems. Taking down a roller furling sail is difficult even in harbour, because of the considerable friction in the luff-spar. Even if you succeed in taking down the sail, setting another one – if you happen to have a second headsail on board

FACT BOX

Roller headsails make life a lot simpler and easier – which is why so many boats fit them. Having said that, if you want to maximise your boat's potential and maintain the ability to make good to windward even when the wind pipes up, at some stage you might want to change the headsail altogether. That's decidedly more difficult with furling gear than it is with a conventional headsail simply hanked to the forestay.

Advantages of roller furling headsails:
- Easy to fit; makes setting and reefing simple.
- When the headsail has been fully furled it leaves the foredeck free and uncluttered, simplifying mooring manoeuvres.
- Setting and furling can be done from the safety of the cockpit.
- The profiled groove which sits over the luff is aerodynamically more efficient than the hanks on a conventional headsail.

Disadvantages of roller furling sails:
- Roller furling gear is expensive – especially if, as I suggest, you also carry several different headsails on board.
- It places more weight in the bows and aloft which increases the boat's tendency to heel and pitch.
- Any mechanism like this has the potential to fail.
- A reefed headsail can't set nearly as well as a conventional headsail and loses its efficiency when sailing upwind.

at all – is equally difficult. The sail has to be fed into the groove of the luff-spar while a second member of the crew hauls in the halyard. And more often than not, cruising boats fitted with roller-furlers only have one general purpose genoa anyway and if you can't use that, you're only left with the main.

But even if the system is working perfectly, there are a number of disadvantages which become evident as soon as you begin to reef the sail in a steadily increasing breeze.

Of course it's much easier to simply roll away a part of the head-sail, than to take down a conventional genoa and replace it with a smaller sail. But your sail has a three-dimensional form: the profile. How can you retain the right shape once the sail has been partly furled?

Sail-makers have come up with the most ingenious ideas to keep the right profile, even in a partly furled sail. Some have highly sophisticated systems which use foam battens behind the luff, some incorporate complicated doubling of the cloth, while others use so-called luff battens which are small, vertical battens along the foot and the leech – all to little avail. As soon as you roll away more than a third of the sail it never really sets properly. It will be full of creases, and the bulky wad around the luff will definitely disturb the flow

of air along the all-important leading edge. If you want to beat to windward in heavy weather with a deeply-reefed roller furling foresail, you'll have to live with the fact that your headsail won't contribute anything towards driving the boat forward. All it does is increase drag and the angle of heel.

◀ A partly furled headsail loses its shape and won't be so effective.

Headsail sizes

The size of your headsail depends largely on the type of rig. As we've seen, these days, the masthead sloop has become so popular that sometimes the alternatives are overlooked. It's undeniably convenient, of course, but there's always a danger that, thanks to modern headsail furling gear, today's sailors will always plump for convenience over efficiency and fail to get the best out their rig. If, on the other hand, your boat has a fractional rig, the emphasis will be slightly different. For a start the headsail triangle will be smaller than it would be on a masthead rig. Incidentally, the headsail triangle is the area between mast and forestay and the length on deck between the front of the mast and the forestay attachment. That's why the fractional rig's larger mainsail plays a more important role. As we've seen, you can trim it to suit a variety of conditions and adapt the sail area to different wind strengths by reefing it rather than changing the headsail. On a well-equipped cruising yacht with a masthead rig and no roller headsail,

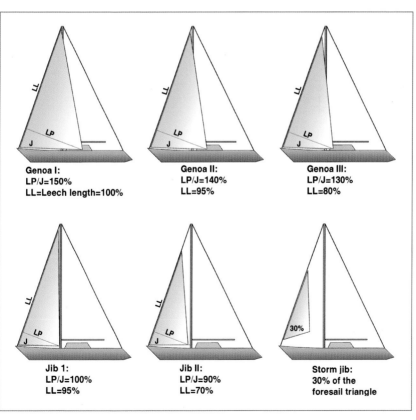

Genoa I:
LP/J=150%
LL=Leech length=100%

Genoa II:
LP/J=140%
LL=95%

Genoa III:
LP/J=130%
LL=80%

Jib 1:
LP/J=100%
LL=95%

Jib II:
LP/J=90%
LL=70%

Storm jib:
30% of the
foresail triangle

the sail wardrobe might include six different jibs and genoas: No 1 genoa, No 2 genoa, No 3 genoa, No 1 jib, No 2 jib and a storm jib. The numbers originated with the IOR rule and are still in use today, even although the IOR rule itself has long ceased to be used in yacht racing.

According to the old IOR, the size of a headsail is defined by its overlap and the ratio of luff length (LL) to forestay length. The overlap can be defined by the luff perpendicular, which is a line that runs from the clew of the sail to the luff where it ends at right angles to it. You now divide the luff perpendicular (LP) by the distance between mast and forestay (J). For example: on a boat whose J is three metres long, a foresail with an LP of 4.5 metres has an overlap of 150 per cent: 4.5 divided by 3 is 1.5.

Clearly, headsails not only differ in size and sail area, but also have different aspect ratios. As we've already seen in the chapter on mainsail trim, a high aspect sail is considerably more effective upwind. On the other hand, a high aspect headsail has to endure much higher stretch stresses than a low aspect sail. A heavy weather sail made from Terylene or Dacron will therefore always have a rather short luff in relation to its foot.

Moreover, different sails have different profiles. A No 3 genoa is much flatter than a No 1 genoa, for example. When the wind increases and you change the headsail, you don't just reduce the sail area, but the depth of the profile as well. This in turn will reduce the angle of heel. That's another reason why you should never only rely on one sail alone, even if you have headsail reefing.

A boat with masthead rig and headsail reefing should ideally carry three headsails on board. A large, deep No 1 genoa with 150 per cent

HEAVY WEATHER

Different headsails are designed to cope with a certain range of wind speeds so you don't have to change them to cope with each minor alteration or every gust. But it's important never to carry too large a sail in strong winds. It not only slows the boat down by increasing the yawing motion and the angle of heel – but also puts the sailcloth under too much stress. It may not rip apart, but at some point could distort and never recover. The shape of the sail will then be permanently destroyed. A No 1 genoa can normally be made to cope with a maximum wind speed of 22 knots while a No 3 genoa might withstand winds of 24 to 32 knots. A large roller furling genoa could also get stressed and damaged if used in heavy weather, even if reefed. Ask your sailmaker to tell you the maximum wind speeds for each sail you carry on board.

overlap, a flatter No 3 genoa with 100 per cent overlap and a luff length of 95 or 100 per cent (which would make it, in effect, a No 1 jib) and a storm jib with a high cut foot.

Tell-tales

This brings us to the fine tuning of the sails themselves, which means it's time to look at the actual trim. To control the flow over the headsail, once again, you need tell-tales. Of course tell-tales only communicate useful and relevant information when you're sailing towards or across the wind. With the wind further aft than amidships, the sails are acting more like scoops. In other words you need a laminar flow on both sides of the sail before a pair of tell-tales can work.

With the mainsail, we're interested in the flow at the tear off edge. That's why the tell-tales are fastened to the leech. The headsail is the first sail in the system so a clear flow at the leading edge is of primary importance. The tell-tales here belong on the front, just behind the luff.

You can find the standard rules for positioning the tell-tales in the fact box on the right.

As a rule of thumb, the tell-tales should be fixed into the sail about 30 to 60 centimetres aft of the luff. At this point, we run into a minor problem. So far, we've assumed that the flow is laminar on both sides of the sail when the angle at which the sail is adjusted to the flow is small. In principle, this still holds true. How-

TELL-TALE TIPS

- In my judgement, you should fit at least three pairs of tell-tales. You can either buy them or make them yourself from cotton or wool. The first should be about a quarter of the luff length below the head of the sail, the second in the middle and the third about a quarter of the luff length above the tack. Some people prefer to fit four pairs but, as I say, three are usually sufficient.

- Each tell-tale should be attached in about the same position as its partner on the other side of the sail so that you can see both flows – the one to windward as well as the one to leeward. However, it's not absolutely essential and you can always move them slightly apart later on if you find that makes it easier to identify each one.

- It's always a good idea to choose a dark colour for the material so the leeward one shines through the sail. If you don't have a roller furling headsail, take care that your tell-tales don't sit directly behind a sail-hank because that might cause turbulence which would only prevent them from working properly.

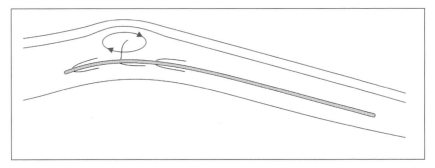

▲ *A small vortex forms immediately behind the luff.*

ever what we now find, if we look at a sail profile in the wind tunnel very closely, is a small amount of turbulence on the lee side just behind the leading edge. This turbulence also manifests itself on the sail. The vortex is important, because without it, there would be no laminar flow across the full width of the sail. The flow needs to tear off at some point in order to create a laminar flow over the rest of the profile. This sounds contradictory, but has been proven in countless wind tunnel tests. On the leeward side just aft of the luff, the sail should have quite a strong radius, to develop lift. Since the flow is unable to follow this radius it tears off in a small vortex which rotates in the direction of the flow. This small vortex is a tiny circulation system in itself and re-directs the airflow back towards the surface of the sail. This particular vortex is the basis which allows the laminar flow to form over the sail in the first place. It must be fairly small so the airflow is laminar over as much area of the sail as possible.

In practice you might just as well ignore the vortex. There's nothing that you can do about it, and anyway it's

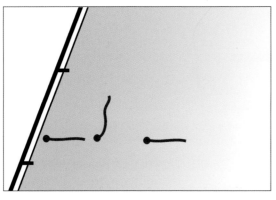

◀ *You can identify the vortex by looking at the tell-tales.*

necessary. But if you happen to fix a tell-tale in that area, it will feed you wrong information. It will flutter about or rise up, even if the flow before and behind the vortex is laminar.

So if you want to be absolutely sure, you should always fix not only one pair of tell-tales, but three in a row and distribute a few of these rows along the luff. The first pair will show a laminar flow if the sail is trimmed correctly. The leeward tell-tale of the second pair will rise, and show the vortex, while the third should again show a perfect laminar flow.

▼ *The tell-tales show:*

a) *Laminar flows to windward and leeward. The sail is developing maximum lift.*

b) *The flow tears off to leeward. The angle is too big because the sail is sheeted in too hard.*

c) *The flow tears off to windward. The angle is too small because the sail has not been sheeted in tight enough.*

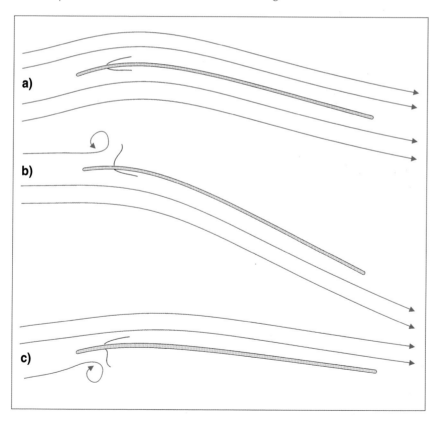

For cruising, it doesn't have to be quite so complicated. In theory you would have to trim your sails very precisely and concentrate hard to make sure you steer a course which gives you three tell-tales flowing evenly to windward with the middle one to leeward rising continuously. In practice, you can merely distribute three or four pairs above each other along the length of the luff and see what they do. If the leeward tell-tales rise or flutter even when you've trimmed your headsail correctly, just re-position them slightly closer to the luff.

Once you've found the best position for the tell-tales, depending on the trim of your sail they will provide you with the following information:

● Tell-tales flowing evenly aft on both sides of the sail, to windward and to leeward. This indicates that the flow across the sail is laminar on both sides and that this is the angle at which the sail delivers maximum lift.
● The tell-tale to windward rises, flutters about or points forward, while the leeward one flows evenly aft. This is an indication that the flow to windward is disturbed because the angle is too small. The sail has not been sheeted in far enough.
● The tell-tale to leeward rises, flutters about or points forward, while the windward one flows evenly aft. This means that the flow

to leeward is disturbed; the angle is too big. The sail has been sheeted in too hard.
● The tell-tale to leeward flows evenly aft, while the one to windward begins to rise from time to time. This shows that the sail is trimmed at the best angle for beating to windward. This angle might not deliver the maximum possible lift, but the best achievable gliding factor – in other words the best ratio between lift and drag.

Forestay tension

To enable the sail to draw properly, we need not only the right angle to the wind, but also the right profile. The same applies here as with the mainsail: the deeper the profile, the more lift, but at the same time that also means more drag. The best ratio of lift and drag will be shown by the tell-tales: the leeward one will flow evenly aft, with the windward one rising from time to time.

The boat's angle of heel is another good indicator. If the tell-tales show that the angle of the sail is correct when sailing upwind, you can reduce the angle of heel by trimming the sail flatter.

The profile can only partly be regulated by tension on the foresail halyard. A tight halyard will put tension on the luff, pull the profile forward and make the sail a little flatter.

Some years ago I tested a sailing boat for one of the yachting maga-

FACT BOX

If the wind blows stronger, it's of fundamental importance that you make sure that your forestay is tight enough. If the forestay is too loose and bends to leeward, you won't be able to sail very close to the wind and the boat will heel too much.

zines. Its carbon fibre mast was unstayed and stepped on the keel. It was mainly held in place by the deck and a forestay was only fitted in order to set a foresail on it. The boat had modern lines with efficient hydrodynamic underwater sections and a fractional rig. On that day we had a fresh breeze and the boat sailed fast and performed well on most points – with one exception: we were unable to sail very close to the wind. The maximum we could achieve was about 50 degrees off the wind; even then the boat would lose a considerable amount of speed. The reason for that can easily be seen in the photograph (pages 76–77): since the mast was completely unstayed apart from the forestay, we were unable to apply any tension to it. Upwind, the forestay was too slack and described a huge curve to leeward. The carbon fibre mast was fairly stiff, but the top third bowed to the thrust of the mainsail and the pull of the forestay. For that reason we had no way of trimming the headsail flat – which is precisely

what we needed to do on a beat in the prevailing conditions. Some unstayed rigs have done away with headsails altogether which is one way of dealing with the problem! On conventional rigs, the best control over the forestay can be achieved with a fractional rig which has running backstays. The tension on the forestay can then easily be regulated by reducing or increasing tension to the windward runner.

If it blows hard, you can put a considerable amount of tension in the windward running backstay. The leeward runner must be left loose to prevent it from chafing along the mainsail. At the same time, you should also pull in the backstay because you want to bend the mast in order to flatten the main. The curvature of the mast can be fine tuned with the trim-stays which are attached to the mast about half way between the running backstays and the boom and which are also connected to the running backstays.

If the wind is light, you need lift to create drive. We already know that a sail with a full, deep profile delivers a lot of lift. If you loosen the backstay, the forestay will bend to leeward. If you now also put some slack into the foresail halyard, the profile will be deeper and move aft.

A slightly loose forestay can also be of advantage if there's a sloppy sea to complement the light wind. The movement of the boat will then disturb the flow at the leading edge of the sail. A loose forestay and thus a fuller sail will be far better able to cope with these disturbances than a flat profile. You will be able to sail less close to the wind, but in such conditions you might be happy to get the boat moving forward at all, rather than to pinch it as close to the wind as possible.

If you have a fractional rig without running backstays and swept-back spreaders, the upper shrouds should be set up tight, as described in the chapter on rig trim. This will transmit tension into the forestay. However, you will have no way of adjusting it while sailing or be able to alter the the profile of the sail to suit the prevailing conditions.

On a masthead rig, the tension on the forestay is only controlled by the backstay. Again, the tension on the backstay, and thus also on the forestay, should be less if the wind is free and light and a choppy sea disturbs the set of the sails. A slack backstay and a consequently slack forestay will help to make the headsail profile deeper and thus more powerful.

▶ *On this unstayed mast, the forestay is loose and bends to leeward. There's no way the boat can sail close to the wind.*

▲ *If the wind is light, the headsail needs to adopt a full and generous profile.*

Some masthead-rigged boats are also fitted with running backstays. If so, the mast will probably have several pairs of spreaders. The curve of the mast can then also be controlled with the running backstays. They will also support the mast in a fore-and-aft direction and stop it from moving when beating in heavy weather into a big sea. Finally, a cutter rig needs running backstays to support the mast at the same point as the second, inner forestay.

Headsail sheet and lead

As before, cruising skippers can learn a lot from their racing counterparts here. With the trend towards ease of handling, there's a slight tendency to think that tuning and trimming is something for obsessives in search of that elusive extra knot and, for that reason, is something best avoided by the sensible and sane. In fact getting your sails to perform efficiently is not only extremely satisfying but can also make a huge difference to the way a boat behaves in a variety of conditions – and with increasingly better fittings on the market it's now all considerably easier. We've already seen the importance of a proper mainsheet traveller to provide flexibility – much the same applies to the headsail which also needs some decent hardware. Of course, when trimming the headsail, the main control line is the sheet. With this, you can regulate the angle and twist of the sail, as well as the depth of the profile. But this can only work if the

▲ *In a fresh breeze, you should trim the headsail as flat as possibly by adjusting the sheet.*

sheet can pull at different angles. The amount of tension you can put on the leech of the foresail depends on how steep an angle the sheet makes at the clew. This in turn regulates the twist. The more tension in the leech, the less twist you will have. For those vital reasons it's important that the lead of the sheet – the block on deck through which it is led aft – can be moved along the deck in a fore-and-aft direction. And that means having a proper track to make the necessary adjustments.

How can you find the right position for the lead? Let's begin with a course upwind and a medium wind strength. Imagine a straight line that begins at right angles to the luff and runs through the clew of the sail towards the deck. Position the lead for the headsail sheet at the point where this imaginary line would meet the deck. Then sheet in the sail until it stops flapping. Look into the sail along the leech and up to the head and make sure that the luff isn't stalling here. Then see how the tell-tales react. If they stream aft only on the lower part of the sail but are fluttering about on the upper part, move the lead forward slightly. If the lower tell-tales flutter and the upper

ones are OK, then move the lead a bit aft. The trim will be right when the tell-tales to the leeward side of the sail stream aft over the entire length of the luff. From time to time, the windward tell-tales should begin to rise upwards; they should be doing this simultaneously in both the lower and upper parts of the sail.

If the wind freshens and the apparent wind is a little freer, you can compensate by luffing up accordingly. At one point, the upper windward tell-tale will begin to flutter permanently and even begin to point forward; after that the sail will stall at that

▲ Upwind, a tight sheet closes the leech of the foresail.

▲ If you bear off and ease off the sheet, the leech will open and the amount of twist in the sail will increase.

point. In this upper part of the sail, because of the twist, the angle will now simply be too small. Also, the profile will be too deep so the boat will begin to heel more. Haul the sheet in tighter, even if it may seem to be straining hard already. In this way you'll pull the sail flat and reduce the twist. You'll also see that the upper tell-tale will calm down at once; heeling will be reduced and the boat will sail faster than it did before.

If the profile in the lower part of the sail no longer changes, even after tightening the sheet further when sailing upwind, you can still gain a little by hauling the sheet in even tighter. But be careful not to take in so much that the leech of the genoa touches the leeward spreader. Chafe here would soon damage the sail; its aerodynamic efficiency would also be reduced if it came into contact with the rig. Also, when you sail upwind and a gust hits the boat and heels it over hard, don't try to resolve the situation by slackening the sheets. On the contrary, you can gain ground to windward. Remember that in a gust, the apparent wind is freer. Because of that, the angle the sails make is too big and, consequently, the boat heels over. You can reduce the angle without touching the sheets at all, simply by turning the entire boat more towards the wind, in other words by luffing up. In this way, you'll make good to windward. For example, if in a true north-westerly wind you can sail 10 degrees on the compass with the wind from your port

side, you might be able to steer true north in a gust. Of course, you'll have to bear off again once the gust has past. If rather than sailing close to the wind you're on a reach, you can change the angle by easing the sheet. However, this will allow the clew to rise and give the sail more twist.

You already know all this because, as we've seen, it also applies to the mainsail, where you control the angle with the traveller and adjust the amount of twist with the mainsheet. With the headsail, there's no traveller so you have to adjust the twist with the lead. If you push the lead forward, the sheet will exert a more vertical pull on the sail; this will tension the leech and reduce twist. If you move the lead aft, the opposite happens: the sheet pulls at an angle and more along the foot of the sail, the leech opens up and the amount of twist increases.

You may at some time or other have heard the rule of thumb that the lead position is correct if both the leech and the foot of the sail don't shake or quiver. It is said that if the leech flutters, the lead must be moved forward while, if the foot is loose, the lead should be moved aft. However, this is hardly a reliable method of trimming the sail. On one hand, the leech and foot of older and tired sails will also flutter when the position of the sheet lead is right, and on the other hand, you can stop every leech from fluttering by simply pulling in the leech-line hard, even if the position of the lead is wrong.

With our tell-tales, we have a far better means of determining the correct trim. You can even use them as an excellent way of fine-tuning the sail. Adjust the lead so the lower tell-tales flow aft evenly. If the lead is too far aft, the upper tell-tales will flutter or point forwards. Move the lead slowly forward until first the middle pair, then the upper pair of tell-tales also stream aft. Now gently and very carefully allow some slack on the sheet, until all the tell-tales to windward rise slowly from time to time.

▲ If the sail has too much twist, it won't work properly and the upper part will be depowered. In strong winds, you can make use of this effect to reduce the angle of heel.

In stronger winds, you can allow more twist in the sail, even if that means the upper part doesn't work effectively anymore. But the centre of effort in the sail will move downwards and the boat will heel less.

Each headsail has different lead positions for each course and each wind strength. On larger yachts you often see two tracks for the lead cars. The forward one is for the jib, the after one for the genoa. After a sail change, remember to change the sheeting position as well. The same applies to a roller furling genoa. If you reef it by winding in part of the sail, you must also correct the sheeting position by moving the lead car. You might even have to change the track.

If you really want to improve trimming efficiency further and make it easier on yourself, you should consider fitting lead cars that can be moved along the track even when under load. Fittings like these would be adjusted with a pulley from the cockpit. If you have a lead car with a snap pin mechanism, there's no way of moving it when it's under load. Having changed the sail, you will have to let out the sheet, after which the sail will flog about while you move the sheet car, before beginning the fine-tuning all over again.

On racing yachts, you might have noticed that they also have parallel tracks on both sides, one further outboard than the other. These serve to change the angle of sheeting in relation to the centreline of the boat.

▲ *Sheeting positions that can be changed while under load are very useful, especially upwind.*

A large No 1 genoa would be sheeted further inboard than a smaller jib in heavy weather. The genoa is a light wind sail that can have more twist because the change of direction of the wind which occurs with increasing height is more pronounced in such conditions – as we've already seen in the chapter about mainsail trim. If the sheeting position is further inboard, you can leave more slack in the sheet, allowing the clew to rise and giving the leech more room to twist. The lead is moved to the outer track if the sail needs to be trimmed flatter and with less twist.

On a reach, it is also useful to be able to adjust the lead position in an athwartships direction. This leaves more scope for fine-tuning the twist. You can also achieve the same result with a barber-hauler. This is a line with a block at the end that rides loosely on the sheet. The line is led outwards to another block on the toe-rail of the boat and back into the cockpit. By pulling on the line, you can move the sheet further outboard and change the sheeting angle without changing the tension on the sheet. This means that the angle can be adjusted without changing the twist. It makes you wonder why no one ever thought of it before.

The inventors of the barber-hauler, by the way, are Manning and Merrit Barber, sailing twins who live in San Diego, California where they have a dental practice.

Strong winds

The stronger the wind blows, the stronger the power that is generated in the sails. As we've already seen, this power can be divided into lift, side force, drag and drive. Unfortunately, the proportion of the useable drive doesn't increase in the same way as the other forces.

A yacht displaces water and creates waves by its movement through the water. With increasing speed, the waves grow bigger and bigger. In other words, the yacht uses up more and more of the overall available energy generated by the sails to make waves. From a certain point onwards, the yacht can sail no faster. It depends on the hull shape and length and is the point where all additional energy goes into the creation of waves. The resistance created by the hull form is like a sound barrier that the boat is unable to break through unless it planes. Once it's reached that limit, which we call displacement hull speed, nothing will make it go any faster.

An average, cruising yacht achieves a hull speed of 2.42 times the square root of its waterline length. Extremely slim hulls like those used on multihulls, reach far higher hull speeds of up to four times the square root of their waterline lengths, because their form resistance is much lower.

As soon as a displacement boat has reached its maximum hull speed, the amount of drive will fail to rise even if the wind increases. Instead the side force will grow dramatically and heeling will increase. This in turn will cause the boat to yaw, which has to be compensated for by increased rudder action – that again slows the boat down.

As the wind increases, you should first try to reduce heel by trimming the sails. Tension the halyards to pull the shape out of them, slide the traveller to leeward and take in the sheets and

▲ *If a boat has reached its hull speed, it remains trapped in its own wave system.*

the kicker. If you have a barber-hauler, use it to pull the sheeting position more outboard and haul in the headsail sheet hard. Finally, move the headsail sheet lead slightly aft to increase twist and thus de-power the upper part of the sail.

Once you've done all that and the boat still heels more than 25 degrees, you'll have to reduce sail area. If you're sailing downwind or on a reach, you might be carrying too much sail without noticing it. The apparent wind would then be less than the true wind and the boat will heel much less than if you were sailing upwind. So on these courses, keep an eye open for changes in the wave pattern and other indications of increasing wind speeds. Don't hesitate to reef early. This is especially important if you're carrying a large downwind sail such as a spinnaker. If you have to take down a sail like that in strong winds, you might break something.

When reducing sail area, begin with the headsail. The next, smaller, genoa is cut flatter and is easier to handle. If you begin to reef the main while holding on to a large genoa, you'll allow the sail's centre of effort to wander forward. This could encourage a tendency to lee helm. As soon as you compensate for lee helm with the rudder, you'll increase leeway and lose your hard-won angle to the wind. In extreme cases, this tendency can be so strong that it's no longer possible to tack through the wind.

If you have a furling headsail, roll it up to the first reef, which should be

▲ *If the boat consistently heels at an angle of more than 25 degrees, you will have to reduce sail.*

marked on the sail. Don't forget to adjust the sheet car accordingly and move it forward to avoid excessive twist in the sail. It's always a good idea to mark the sheeting positions for the different sizes of sail on the track.

If your roller furling genoa is not one that takes kindly to reefing, you will now have to change down to the next smaller-sized sail. At sea and in rough weather this is a difficult job. If, at the outset, you expect the wind to increase later on during a passage, you might be better off by setting a smaller sail in the first place – in the harbour, before you leave. If you set conventional headsails on sail hanks, you'll have to change the sail anyway.

Sooner (if you have a fractional rig) or later (if you have a masthead rig) it will be time to reef the mainsail.

While a well-equipped, sea-going yacht might carry six or more different headsails on board, in all probability you'll only have one mainsail. This is the sail that would be used in light airs as well as in a gale. This of course means that you'll need to have a means of reducing its area effectively to make it suitable for different wind speeds.

The first step in every reefing manoeuvre is to let the pressure off the sail. This is where beginners often make a serious mistake. Don't turn the boat head-to-wind. Apart from the fact that it will probably be impossible to keep the yacht head-to-wind without using the engine, the flogging mainsail will be very difficult to reef. The flogging headsail will very prob-

ably be damaged in the rigging too, especially if it's made of expensive Mylar or Kevlar. It's much more effective to sail close to the wind with a well trimmed, flat headsail and to let out the mainsail only to the point where it de-powers without flogging over its entire length.

If there's enough sea room, you can also heave-to to reef. This is a time-honoured manoeuvre which is simple to perform and extremely effective. It's done by tacking from an upwind course but leaving the jib sheet belayed. The jib will now be aback on the new windward side and the boat will try to bear off. The rudder is now turned hard to weather (tiller to lee or wheel to windward) and fixed in that position. The boat

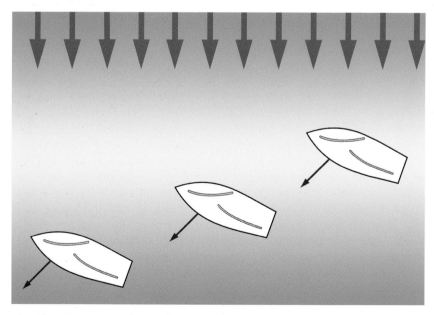

▲ When hove-to, your boat will slowly drift to leeward and be relatively stable.

will settle a bit closer to the wind than abeam and slowly drift to leeward. It's a good idea to try heaving-to before you really need to because every boat responds slightly differently. Some long-keelers settle down at once; other, more modern boats can be a bit twitchy and sensitive. The advantage of heaving-to is that you won't have to steer – not only that, the boat will be surprisingly steady even in heavy seas. Having heaved-to, it's relatively easy to take in a reef or two. If you need to reef when running downwind, don't let out the mainsheet, because that will only increase the pressure in the sail. Instead, tighten the kicking strap or boom vang as much as possible, take the boom amidships with the sheet and then reef.

Sensible sail handling in strong winds has a great deal to do with anticipation and planning ahead. That's why it's so important to get regular weather checks and prepare for the worst. It's particularly dangerous to hang on to your sails for too long – and then run into serious problems when you try to change them. Going forward in heavy seas is often hazardous and heaving foredecks are dangerous places – particularly if you have to haul down a thrashing headsail. Prudent skippers therefore try to keep one step ahead – not just by changing down before heavy weather hits but also making sure that all the necessary equipment is in place and ready to hand.

Reef points and storm trysails

The oldest and probably the simplest way of reefing is to use reef points or lines. In days gone by, sails were pulled down by hand and the excess canvas, or bunt, tied up with lengths of line sewn into the sail on either side like a parcel. You can still see crews on yard-arms doing much the same thing on square riggers today. Reefing lines are still found on a huge number of boats but modern versions consist of a number of eyelets sewn into the luff and the leech of the sail, in line with each other, and at various heights. The reefing lines would be fixed to one side of the end of the boom and led through one of the eyelets in the leech, then from there back to a block on the other side of the boom and from that point forward to the mast and the reefing winch.

The blocks on the boom should be positioned aft of the reefing eye to give an angled pull. In practice, with the reef pulled down, they should make a straight line with the reefing eye and a point about half way up the luff of the sail. In practice, therefore, each reef has a two-part pulley with which the leech and the foot of the reefed sail can both be tightened by the same amount. In that way, the profile of the sail is flattened over its entire width. When taking in a reef, you don't only reduce the actual sail area but also adapt the shape to suit the new conditions.

Normally there would be three rows of reefing eyes in the mainsail, which means you can reef three times. The procedure starts by taking in the topping lift a bit to support the boom and to open up the leech. If you don't have a topping lift, you could always use the spinnaker halyard instead. Then slacken off the mainsheet and loosen the halyard until you can slip the eyelet in the luff over the hook fitting on the gooseneck. The eyelet now becomes the tack of the reefed sail. If the sail flogs about too hard, it can be quite a tough job. So, if hooking the eyelet over the fitting proves too difficult, just take in the sheet a bit to calm the sail down.

As soon as the eyelet is hooked, tighten the halyard until the luff is taut enough again. Only now should you pull in the reefing line on the end of the boom that pulls down the leech. If you try to do it before the halyard is tight again, you'll only pull the luff out of the mast groove.

In the old days, people traditionally tied down the reefed sail to the boom using small grommets which were sown into the sail. The trouble was, however, that this would only make the sail baggier, which in turn generated more drag and made the boat heel. In modern reefing systems, as we've seen, the problem has been solved by positioning the after reefing blocks on the boom to ensure that the sail gets pulled both down and aft at the same time. This simple innovation has made reefing grommets more or less redundant because, rather than having to tie up the superfluous cloth, or bunt, with pennants or points you can merely let it lie loosely over the boom.

Of course you can still use grommets to tie the cloth down to the boom if you want to. However, it's worth remembering that they were

▲ Using the modern type of reefing line, you can not only easily reduce the sail area of the mainsail, but also change its profile and make it flatter.

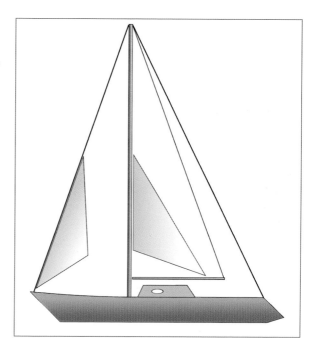

▶ *A storm jib and a storm trysail should be standard equipment on an ocean-going yacht.*

never designed to take large stresses and you should always undo them before shaking out a reef, otherwise you might pull them out of the sail.

The two-part reefing tackle on the leech can also be rigged in such a way that it runs along the boom to the gooseneck, then through a block, up through the reefing eyelet in the luff, then down again to a winch or, better still, straight back to the cockpit. You now have a single-line reefing system which can save you from having to go to the mast in order to reef and to pull the luff eyelet over the hook fitting. Now, all you have to do is loosen the mainsail halyard and at the same time take in the reefing line. That will pull the sail down to the boom and make it flatter. The line should be tightened

as hard as possible using a winch, because it's bound to stretch a little after a while. This would encourage some shape back into the main, which is something we want to avoid in conditions when the wind is strong enough to reef.

In my opinion, the single-line reefing system is superior to every other reefing system. It means you can reef quickly and from the safety of the cockpit and, as long as your winches are sufficiently powerful, without too much effort. As a welcome bonus, the reefed main will have a flat profile and set well. Last but not least, the whole system is easy to fit and is relatively inexpensive. It would be a good idea if production boatbuilders fitted it as standard.

Of course, if it blows really hard you might be left with no other option than to take down all the sails and run before the wind under bare poles. This of course could only be undertaken if there were enough sea room to leeward. This is a passive storm tactic and only really works well if your boat is a more traditional shape with a long, deep keel. Such hull forms make it easier to keep the boat stern to wind and sea when there's no help from the sails. In contrast, modern light displacement yachts with their cutaway underbodies and short keels need to be actively sailed for as long as possible. In big and breaking seas, this type of boat has a much bigger tendency to broach than the more traditional designs. On a modern boat, you would set a storm jib and reef the main as deeply as possible. Or, better still, you could take down the main and hoist a storm trysail instead.

Storm trysails are unfashionable now – at least on your average, modern cruising yacht. However, most long-distance and blue-water boats still carry them. The trysail is an out-and-out storm sail. It's cut very flat and made of extremely heavy cloth. The leech is straight and carries no battens. This sail should ideally be set in its own track on the mast. If the track runs right down to the deck, you can stow the sail in its bag at the foot of the mast and leave it bent on which means you can set it in extreme conditions without having to hank it on first. More importantly, if the trysail has its own separate track,

you won't have to remove the mainsail in order to use it.

The trysail is always set loose-footed and rather than being sheeted via the boom, is led aft. For that reason, the boom can then be fixed in one position and lashed down on deck to eliminate what could be a serious potential source of injury in heavy weather; a wildly swinging boom is extremely dangerous. Incidentally, the area of the trysail would only be about a quarter of the size of the un-reefed mainsail.

Under storm jib and storm trysail, you won't be able to sail very close to the wind. You will, however, be able to lay a course to the wind a few degrees better than abeam. That's important because it means that the bows, the strongest part of the boat, will take the main force of oncoming seas. The sails will also help stabilise the boat and dampen any rolling. And if you don't have enough sea-room to leeward for comfort, you should at least be able to hold your ground rather than drifting backwards.

However, as long as you're not planning any really long ocean passages, you'll probably always be able to avoid really serious weather conditions. The modern cruising skipper has access to an excellent variety of reliable weather-forecast information sources which can also be received when under way, and if bad weather is in the offing, there will probably always be enough time to seek shelter in the nearest harbour.

In-boom reefing

The idea of reefing the main by simply rolling it around the boom goes back a long way. A sail which is reefed in this fashion is unlikely to set very well at all, and tends to be very full because there's no way of tensioning the foot while the sail is actually reefed. Furthermore, the force of the wind will also curve the leech forward. As an alternative, modern in-boom reefing systems consist of a hollow spar with a rotating axle in the middle. The end of the boom carries a roller on which the reefing line is wound up when you set the sail. The line itself is led inside the boom to the gooseneck, down the mast and aft into the cockpit.

Handling such a system needs a certain amount of care. When setting the main, you have to feed in the reefing line as you haul on the halyard so it gets wound up neatly on the roller and doesn't foul up. Conversely, when you reef or hand the main, you have to pull in the reefing line while simultaneously easing the halyard, which must be kept in tension and under control. Otherwise, the main could come down too quickly, in which case it would be impossible to roll it neatly around the axle inside the boom, and instead the whole thing would jam up.

It's essential to have a fully battened main if you want this kind of system because the lower battens must keep tension on the foot of the sail when it's reefed. Foot tension can only be adjusted when the sail is fully

out, after that you rely entirely on the battens. Since you reef from batten to batten, it's only the tension of the lower batten that keeps the profile of the sail flat.

In order to reef and roll up the sail inside the boom without any creases, the luff and foot of the sail must always form more or less a right angle to each other. This necessitates a rigid kicking strap that supports the boom while the sail is reefed, and a

▲ *This in-boom reefing gear has a rotating axle inside a hollow spar around which the sail is wound.*

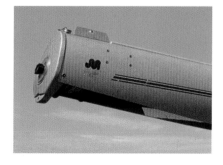

▲ *The reefing line is wound around a drum at the end of the boom. You can also see a small adjusting screw which can alter the tension of the foot.*

▲ Top left: *Here a special groove keeps the luff at the right distance from the mast.*

▲ Top right: *Full-length battens help the main to keep its profile even in very light airs.*

▲ Above left: *The halyard is led through two fairleads at the top of the mast. A distance spacer sits in the original mast track and can be made of plastic or cloth. In harbour, this fitting can make a vibrating noise in high winds. You can sometimes stop this by wrapping the main halyard around the mast. Alternatively, you might dispense with it and rivet a fixed aluminium strip to the back of the mast instead; however, that would be more expensive.*

block and tackle to stop it rising up when sailing.

When setting the main, you have to keep the boat as nearly head-to-wind as possible. Otherwise, the battens could jam inside the boom or foul the rigging.

Of course, it's not just boats with in-boom reefing that need to be kept head-to-wind when hoisting or lowering; it also applies to any boat with a fully-battened main. With in-boom systems the battens are kept under fairly high tension so they can stretch the sail flat after reefing. Accordingly, it takes strength to set the sail, because you have to

overcome the friction of the battens along the entire length of the luff. For that reason I would only recommend fitting an in-boom reefing system on boats whose mainsail luffs are not much longer than, say, 12 metres. After that, the extra stress of setting the sail offsets any handling advantages there might be when you decide to reef.

Most in-boom reefing systems can be fitted to existing masts. You will of course need a new boom with its own furling mechanism as well as a new track on the mast for the luff of the mainsail. The old mast track will no longer be suitable because the luff

▲ *When reefed, the lower batten has to maintain tension in the foot of the sail. This only partially works.*

needs to be set back from the mast so you can roll it into the boom. A special fitting at the top of the mast provides a similar space for the halyard.

Advantages of an in-boom reefing system compared to an in-mast reefing system:

- Boom, mast track and kicker can be retro-fitted.
- With a fractional rig, the main can be trimmed flatter because the mast can still be bent, even with in-boom reefing.
- The sail has a larger area and will set nicely even in light airs because of the battens.
- The additional weight of the reefing mechanism is located close to the boat's centre of gravity so you don't increase the weight aloft.
- If the reefing mechanism fails, it's still easy to take down the mainsail.

Disadvantages of the in-boom reefing:

- The friction of the battens calls for a certain amount of effort when hoisting the sail.
- The boom is fairly heavy and increases the risk of injury to the crew during uncontrolled gybes.
- Once the foot of the sail has been tensioned, it can't be adjusted any more, especially when the sail is reefed.
- The sail can only be hoisted, reefed or taken down when the boat is exactly head-to-wind.
- Reefing in strong winds means you may be dependent on your engine.

The sails will flog during reefing which can damage the cloth. The headsail is particularly prone to this.

- It's essential to have an efficient and reliable rigid kicker because the boom must be kept at right angles to the mast when you hoist, reef or lower the sail.
- In harbour, the new mast track can make annoying and anti-social noises in high winds.

In-mast reefing

Some in-mast reefing systems can be fitted as add-ons to existing rigs. Such devices usually consist of a hollow profile, which would be riveted to the after end of your mast. As before, the centre of the tube carries a revolving axle around which the mainsail will be rolled. The reefing line is led around a large drum located beneath the gooseneck fitting. The drum is connected to the rotating axle.

The mainsail is set with an outhaul-line attached to a car, which runs freely along the boom. From here, the line is led through an integrated block in the sail's clew to the end of the boom, back inside the boom to the mast and aft into the cockpit. Since you set the sail by taking in the outhaul, the reefing line gets wound automatically onto the reefing drum. To reef the sail or to take it in completely, all you need to do is pull on the reefing line, which in turn will roll up the sail inside the mast tube. That means you only need to handle one line at a time for setting, reefing

▲ *The outhaul pulls the mainsail out of the hollow profile which is fitted to the after side of the mast.*

▲ *The reefing line runs around a spindle or dum that sits below the gooseneck.*

or taking in the sail. Both outhaul and reefing line would be led to the cockpit and fed through halyard locks, then onto a self-tailing winch. The area of the mainsail is infinitely variable. Using the winch, you can then tension the foot of the sail to make it nice and flat.

Obviously, it's impossible to fit horizontal battens in the sail, because you would not then be able to roll the sail up inside the mast tube. The leech of the main must therefore be cut straight or even hollow. Vertical battens are one alternative but they only allow a very slight curvature of the leech.

The new hollow mast profile adds weight, needs stronger rigging and stiffens the mast – which means you won't be able to bend it to adjust the shape of the mainsail any more. The mainsails on in-mast reefing systems are always smaller than conventional mains and cut fairly flat. To a limited extent, the profile of the sail will adjust to the prevailing wind by itself: if the main is completely unfurled, the axle inside the tube will be somewhat loose and in turn allow the sail a slightly 'negative' luff curve, making it fuller. As you reef and furl the sail around the axle, it becomes stiffer and the shape becomes flatter. The precise shape and degree of angle and twist are controlled by the traveller, kicker and mainsheet.

The mainsail of an in-mast reefing system will deliver less lift and more drag than a conventional sail, That's because, to start with, the sail is

▲ *Vertical battens in the leech only allow a very slight roach.*

smaller, the leech less curved or not rounded at all, and the profile flatter. The foot is set loose, so the pressure compensation can freely flow around it. That, in turn, causes disturbance of the flow and induced resistance.

As already intimated, an in-mast reefing system also adds considerable weight aloft, reducing the yacht's overall stability. It follows, therefore, that a sea-going cruising yacht needs to have a certain amount of reserve stability in order to be able to carry such a rig safely. Like some

other modern devices, it's undeniably ingenious but as with most things there's a price to pay.

Advantages of in-mast reefing vs in-boom reefing:

- It's fairly easy to handle without much effort because you only use one line at a time.
- The sail can be set, reefed and taken in on any point of sailing, even when running dead downwind.
- The outhaul allows you to adjust the profile of the sail within certain limits by tensioning the foot of the sail.
- You don't need a rigid kicker.

Disadvantages of in-mast reefing systems:

- The area of the main is smaller and its profile flatter. This causes a loss in drive especially when sailing on a reach or downwind.
- The system adds more weight aloft.
- You can't use horizontal battens, so an aerodynamically desirable curvature of the leech is impossible. In light airs, the profile will simply flap and collapse as soon as there's any swell.
- If the mechanics of the system should fail, there's no way of taking down the sail. Repairing the mechanism on board with limited tools and facilities may be impossible.

Downwind sailing

Much of our research so far has shown how even small alterations to our rig and sails can make a big difference. We also know that sails work differently when running before the wind rather than sailing towards it. Upwind, lift and drag work against each other and the sails must be trimmed in such a way that they deliver maximum lift and minimum drag. When running downwind, lift and drag both act in the same direction. It follows, therefore, that on freer courses the amount of lift that drives the boat becomes less while the drag factor increasingly takes over as the boat's driving force. The sails should now be trimmed to produce as much drag as possible.

Sailing upwind, you need a flat sail shape that produces little drag and has a high aspect ratio, while the area itself can be relatively small. Reaching or running, you need sails with as much area as possible and as deep a profile as possible.

Of course you can also use your upwind sails to run downwind. But if you do, you'll reduce your boat's potential, especially if the wind is only light to moderate. On such courses it's much more efficient to set specially designed downwind sails.

You'll also have to use the main when running as well. A modern Bermudian mainsail isn't particularly effective downwind so theoretically it would make sense to change it for a gaff when running, but, of course, that would be impractical.

Headsails are considerably more flexible. You can take down your genoa or jib and set a specially designed downwind sail in its place: a spinnaker, gennaker, cruising chute or blister – so let's take a detailed look at the options.

Spinnakers

The spinnaker remains the most widely used downwind sail of all. For some skippers, this colourful 'kite', usually made from lightweight nylon, is a fun challenge; others, on the other hand, try to avoid using it altogether because they find it far too difficult to handle.

The origin of the name 'spinnaker' by the way is unclear and the topic of many heated discussions among the experts. Some believe it to be a derivation of the term 'spin-maker'. Others insist that it can be traced back to the name of the British yacht

▲ *Running under spinnaker downwind, a flat-bottomed, dinghy-like hull can break through the physical restrictions which apply to a displacement boat and plane at more than its hull speed.*

▲ *Radial head spinnakers are widely used on cruising boats.*
Tri-radial spinnakers are more complex to make and mainly used on racing boats.

Sphinx which was the first to set such a sail, then called a 'balloon-jib', back in the year 1866.

These early downwind sails of the 19th century had little in common with the modern spinnakers we know today. They, too, were cut very full and were poled out, but those are just about the only things in common. They were also cut asymmetrically like all the other headsails. The larger these balloon sails were, the more difficult they became to handle.

Eventually, experiments began with symmetrical spinnakers. The first designs emanated from the New York sail loft of Ratsey & Lapthorn. They were like an inverted 'V' with a pointed head. The cloth ran parallel to the two leeches.

The next generation of spinnakers were cut more roundly, had more sail area, and more closely resembled an inverted 'U'. They were made from weft-oriented cloth which ran parallel to the foot of the sail.

The panels of cloth on modern spinnakers run along the lines of the greatest stresses. In a radial-headed spinnaker, the upper panels are laid out like spokes in a wheel, but run horizontally in the lower part of the sail. Tri-radial spinnakers are made from warp-oriented cloth that runs in panels from the head, the clew and the tack of the sail towards the centre. This sail is extremely strong and can also be used in fresh winds. Racing sailors generally prefer tri-radial spinnakers.

Spinnaker gear

Unlike jibs or genoas, spinnakers are set flying. Only the three corners – head, tack and clew – are actually connected to the boat. The sail is hoisted and set with the spinnaker halyard attached to the sail's head. The tack is set up on a fitting at the outboard end of the spinnaker pole while the leeward sheet holds the clew. The inner end of the spinnaker boom is attached to the mast in a fitting that allows the boom to be swung around to the other side of the boat.

Unlike jibs or genoas, spinnakers aren't attached to the forestay. Instead, a spinnaker pole holds the luff of the sail to windward of the mast so the sail can be set in an area away from aerodynamic disturbance created by the main. A line, known as the guy, is fastened to the outboard end of the spinnaker pole which is also where the tack of the spinnaker sits. The guy adjusts the angle of the pole to the apparent wind.

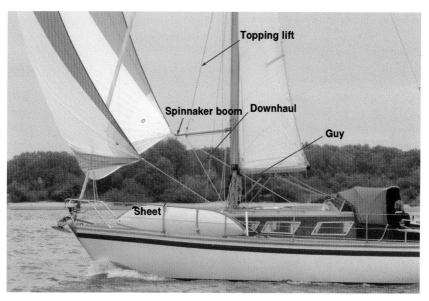

▶ Spinnaker gear.

Both spinnaker sheets – the guy and the sheet – must be led outside and around the boat's running and standing rigging. They are then led aft through two blocks to winches in the cockpit.

Two further lines are fastened about half way along the spinnaker pole and serve to adjust its horizontal position. The topping lift is used to support the boom at the right height; the downhaul prevents it from rising up too far.

Since the spinnaker is cut symmetrically, both tack and clew, as well as the two side leeches, will have the same form and cut. Depending from which side the wind blows, they change names and functions. The windward leech becomes the luff and the windward corner the tack, while the leeward leech remains the leech and the leeward corner is the clew. During a gybe, the boom is brought over to the other side of the boat and the new tack fastened to its outboard end. To do that, the boom is either taken from its mast fitting, or pulled upwards at the mast end and swung around behind the forestay.

The aerodynamics of a spinnaker

Your main, jib and genoa will normally be trimmed to achieve a 100 per cent flow across the sails. The spinnaker works in a somewhat different way. For a start, it's considerably deeper so the flow can never be expected to follow the entire width of the sail; it's bound to tear off sooner

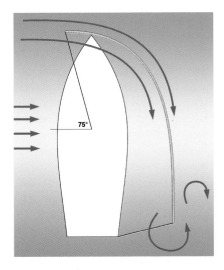

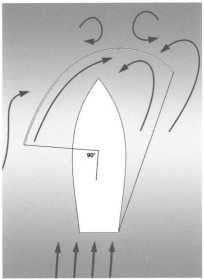

▲ Top: *On a reach or with the wind abeam, the flow will tear off after coming into contact with about 50 per cent of the sail area.*

Below: *Running downwind, the flow will tear off completely.*

or later. If you sail on a reach with the apparent wind at about 120 to 90 degrees off the boat's centreline, the flow will probably tear off half way across the sail behind the luff. To help keep the flow laminar across even this small part of the sail, you need to trim the spinnaker as flat as possible. To do that, you need to swing the boom forward until it sits at roughly 75 degrees to the apparent wind. The tearing off of the flow also generates drag at right angles to the boat's direction which, in turn, will heel it over and reduce its speed. The more the wind moves forward, the bigger this negative component will become. As soon as you try to sail on a point with the wind any further forward than amidships, a spinnaker ceases to be effective at all and may even be a positive handicap so, at that point, you should then change it for your genoa or jib.

Running downwind, the flow will tear off directly behind the leeches. However, the induced drag now begins acting in the direction of the boat's forward motion. The boom is at a right angle to the apparent wind. Drag, kinetic pressure to windward of the spinnaker and a loss in pressure in its lee will all help to move the boat forwards. The wind gets reflected along the curve of the spinnaker and flows around the leeches in a wide arc. This phenomenon increases the effective sail area and is even more pronounced if the sail is trimmed flatter.

Setting the spinnaker

During a race, a host of factors determine the precise moment at which the spinnaker should be set. If, for example, after a beat to the windward mark, the next leg is a dead run, it means rounding the mark, bearing off, perhaps also gybing and at the same time swiftly hoisting the spinnaker. Not surprisingly therefore, handling the big sail needs understanding and expertise. Cruising skippers can take more time and choose the best moment to hoist. You steer the boat on a course where the wind is from behind, but not dead downwind. You then take down the headsail, rig the spinnaker pole and the sheets, before hoisting the spinnaker in the lee of the mainsail.

When you hoist the spinnaker, set the pole up so it's horizontal and nearly touching the forestay. Once

PRACTICAL TIP

When sailing shorthanded, you can make things considerably easier by hoisting the spinnaker in the blanketing lee of the foresail. The mainsail alone won't be big enough to keep the wind out of the huge spinnaker. You need to have another cleat for the headsail sheet in the cockpit because you'll want both sheet winches for the spinnaker. Make sure that the sheet doesn't get tangled in the extra cleat when sailing upwind.

the sail has been hoisted, haul the tack of the sail around the forestay, until it touches the end of the pole, by hauling in the windward sheet, which in this case is the guy. The pole's downhaul must be tight and belayed. With the sheet to leeward, you haul the clew of the sail back until it nearly reaches the cockpit. In this way, tack and clew are pulled far apart and the sail has less chance to get twisted around either itself or the forestay. Normally, all you now have to do to fill it with wind is to take down the jib or genoa, if still set, or pull the spinnaker back with the guy until it fills.

Trimming the spinnaker

Once the sail is full of wind, you need to fine-tune it. A spinnaker is a rather unstable creature which can adopt a huge variety of different shapes. Its leading edge along the luff is formed only by the wind rather than by a forestay. For that reason, it takes experience to find the right trim and you'll only get the best from your spinnaker if you try it out in moderate winds as often as you can. Above all, it's worth remembering the old adage that practice makes perfect. Sailing with a spinnaker is really satisfying once you get the hang of it.

Here are a few general rules:
- If the wind is from dead astern to about 120 degrees off the centre-line, you can trim the leeches best if the boom is at right angles to the apparent wind. If the wind is any

▲ *The spinnaker begins to fill.*

▲ *Using the guy, trim the spinnaker boom until the sail is full with only the luff still collapsing.*

further forward than 120 degrees, you should trim the sail flat to try and keep a laminar flow over the largest part of the sail. As we've seen in the previous chapter, to do that, you trim the pole so it has an angle of 75 degrees to the apparent wind.

- To tune the sail, first trim the guy and belay it. You can then always correct the angle of the flow with the (leeward) sheet. Since the flow will always tear off when running downwind, tell-tales make no sense on a spinnaker. However, the shape of the luff is quite interesting. If the angle is too large, the luff will be in a zone of turbulence. If it's too small the speed of the flow to windward and leeward, as well

▲ *Finally take in the sheet until the luff stops curling up.*

as the pressures, will be the same. In both cases, the luff will collapse or begin to curl up.

- To find the correct angle, take in the sheet until the spinnaker is full. Then let out the sheet very carefully until the point is reached where the luff just begins to curl. Continuously check the angle by 'playing' the sheet, otherwise the moment you get it wrong, the heeling force will slow the boat down dramatically.

- The shape of the leech is also controlled by the sheet, or rather by the sheeting position. A sheeting position further aft opens up the leech and de-powers the sail. This can be helpful on a reach and especially in strong winds. If you want to increase the power of the sail, move the sheeting position forward and by doing so close the leech. Adjusting the sheet can have a detrimental effect on the shape of an unstable spinnaker. That can partly be avoided by trimming the end of the pole in relation to the height of the clew. To see whether you've got it right, look at the luff. Observe closely and find out in which part of the sail the luff begins to curl up first when you let out the sheet. If it happens in the upper part of the sail, the pole must be trimmed too low and needs to be adjusted with the topping lift. If the luff curls up in the lower part of the sail, the end of the pole is too high and needs to be pulled down with the down-

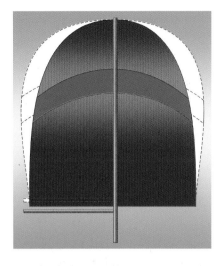

◀ If you lift the boom, the leeches will be further apart and the sail will be flatter.

haul. If the boom is at the correct height, the luff will start to curl half way up the sail.

- The height of the pole controls the depth of the spinnaker's profile. The higher the tack and clew are trimmed, the more the luff and the leech of the sail can be blown apart by the wind and the flatter the profile will be. If, on the other hand, you move the boom downwards, the leech and luff will move closer, their distance to each other will be decreased and the depth of the sail accordingly increased.

Spinnaker problems

Having said that a spinnaker can be fun, it's equally important to point out some of the potential problems if you mishandle it. For a start, the spinnaker is the sail with the largest area so, not surprisingly, as the wind gets stronger it can get increasingly difficult to handle. A spinnaker will push the sail's centre of effort a long way forward and upwards. The wind will also use the mast as a lever and push the bow into the water and the stern will lift.

Up to a certain point, such a bows-down trim can actually make a boat sail faster but if the wind really blows, things can also quickly get out of hand. The waves that push the boat along from behind will have a tendency to make the boat broach when the stern is still accelerating as a result of the oncoming wave, and the bow in the trough is being slowed down. This tendency is increased if the bow is trimmed deep into the water. Also, the further the stern is lifted, the less grip the rudder will have and the less chance you have of trying to steer your way out of a potential broach. If that happens, the boat will slew round and end up with the wind abeam. For racing skippers

PRACTICAL TIP

If your boat begins to roll, don't try and compensate by steering your way out of it. On the contrary, steer towards the direction in which the boat heels. Bear off when the spinnaker starts pulling you to leeward and luff up when it pulls to windward. If the yacht rolls or heels so much that you can't steer her properly any more, release the sheet. The end of the sheet should be free to run through the blocks and should never have a stopping knot on it. The clew will flap to leeward and any pressure will quickly disappear. Never let go of the guy. The boom could swing forward until it hits the forestay and stops there. The sail would still have wind in it and pull the boat hard over to leeward, which could even capsize it.

it's fairly common but cruising skippers can adopt a more prudent approach.

If the wind increases, you should first trim the sail flatter by moving the sheet leads further forward. Otherwise, downwind the spinnaker will multiply the boat's rolling motion until it becomes uncontrollable. Large areas of turbulence break off along the leeches of the spinnaker. Wind tunnel testing has shown that this doesn't happen all at once, but alternates from one side to the other. These periodically changing areas of turbulence now create side forces which cause a swinging motion across the wind. This in turn will make the boat roll.

The rolling motion will be amplified by the fact that the leech in the downward roll has a sideways flow across it. Since the apparent wind speeds are relatively small when running, the fast sideways movement when rolling creates an effective flow across the leech which is now effectively the 'leading edge'; this in

turn will again create aerodynamic lift. This force works in the direction of the boat's roll and if this aero-dynamically animated rolling isn't offset by the boat's lateral plan, it will soon reach a point where the boat is completely out of control. The boat will have very strong weather helm and will finally become un-steerable and broach, with the spinnaker pulling the boat sideways and flat onto the water. Modern hulls, with their small underwater areas, are particularly prone.

Venturi spinnaker

In an attempt to dampen the yawing motions of a modern yacht under spinnaker, the Venturi spinnaker was developed in the 1950s. It was named after the Italian physicist Giovanni Batista Venturi (1765 to 1822) who discovered that inside a quickly flowing medium a suction or slipstream develops as a result of the pressure decrease against the stationary surroundings.

The surface of a Venturi spinnaker has countless tiny holes in it, on the leeward side of which little 'jets' of cloth are sewn. They should accelerate the flow of air to the leeward side of the spinnaker and re-direct it downwards. This accelerated flow should create the suction discovered by Venturi and thus increase the drive of the sail. It was also hoped that the phenomenon would create a stabilising effect on the sail at the same time.

However, the Venturi spinnaker has never proved itself in practice. The tiny cloth jets do indeed increase the resistance value of the sail so that it develops more driving force than its conventional counterpart, but there's no stabilising effect. On the contrary: the increased pressure drop on the leeward side of the sail only serves to push the bow down even deeper into the water than before. This of course increases the risk of broaching. As an added drawback, the Venturi spinnaker is notoriously difficult to take down, especially in gusts, Even if the guy has been completely released, the sail will still remain at least partly full of wind because of the numerous little jets.

Parasail

So, the spinnaker is undeniably effective, but can it be fundamentally improved? Above all can it be adapted to prevent the bows from digging in? The parasail is a relatively new development which arrived on the market around 2001

and which, on the face of it, seems to have solved some of the long-term basic problems associated with conventional spinnakers. Not surprisingly then, the parasail has been developed primarily to lighten the bows of the boat and therefore enhance the steering capability; it also aims to stabilise the boat and resist the rolling momentum. The idea is the brainchild of the sailor and paraglide-flyer Hartmut Schädlich. Together with the paraglide-engineer Manfred Kistler and Arne Wehrlin he developed a symmetrical spinnaker with a huge gap running across the upper half. In front of this opening, a 'parachute' is suspended by a system of fine lines.

The air flows through the gap and over the parachute at a small angle. This angle and the shape are determined by the lines and can't be changed.

If the wind blows at Beaufort force 3 or more, the parachute will unfold. It then acts like a wing and creates lift which is directed upwards and forwards. The parachute not only pulls the sail along and increases its drive, but also lifts the spinnaker and in turn also takes load off the bows.

This effect has been proven in wind tunnel tests. The pressure on the bow of a yacht sailing with the parasail is measurably less than one sailing with a conventional spinnaker. And the difference becomes more pronounced the stronger the wind blows. In a force 6, the pressure on the bow is about 20 per cent less than if the boat were flying a

▲ *The main feature of the parasail is the gliding parchute which stabilises the boat and provides forward lift.*

which the sailcloth began to tear. While a conventional spinnaker would start to roll uncontrollably from force 8 onwards, the parasail remained completely steady. There's another point worth noting: the size of the gap in the sail is about 15 per cent of the overall area. Because the air flows through this gap without being 'used', they were worried at first that the resistance value of the sail would be reduced by the same amount. However, precise measurements showed that the loss in resistance value of the parasail against a conventional spinnaker was only between one and 1.5 per cent.

The stabilising effect of the parasail will undoubtedly also increase the speed of the boat. The rolling motion causes turbulence around the keel and other underwater appendages, and the induced resistance here will slow the boat down considerably. A boat that sails along steadily without rolling will cause much less resistance through the water and thus sail correspondingly faster.

conventional spinnaker. In addition, the lift created in the sail stabilises it and also helps the boat resist the dreaded rolling momentum. The effect can be likened to a huge, invisible hand holding the mast of the boat steady. This is an effective method of counteracting the aerodynamically enhanced rolling motion of the boat, which will now remain under complete control even in extremely strong and gusty winds.

Schädlich and his partners have tested the sail in the wind tunnel for wind speeds up to 100 kilometres per hour (Beaufort force 10), after

Cruising chutes

Many cruising sailors shy away from using the spinnaker because they think it is simply too complicated to handle. Finding space for an extra spar on the foredeck, for example, is a nuisance, as is the need to trim additional sheets. Moreover, the spinnaker is a pure downwind sail

▲ *A blister or cruising chute can't cope with too much pressure on the sheet and will lose its shape. The depth of its profile is regulated by the luff.*

and must be changed for a genoa as soon as the wind is abeam or forward of amidships.

There are several alternatives. You could try a less unwieldy asymmetric spinnaker which still needs a pole, or alternatively, a light, full bodied headsail usually referred to as a cruising chute or blister. Compared to a conventional spinnaker, the main difference here lies in its asymmetrical cut. Luff and leech have different shapes and tack and clew stay on the same side on all points. Finally, the sail is normally smaller than a spinnaker. Tri-radial cruising chutes offer more performance than radial head alternatives and allow you to sail closer to

the wind, but a radial head chute is easier to handle.

The luff of the chute is longer than the forestay and the profile considerably deeper than that of a genoa. Like the spinnaker, the chute is also set flying, but you don't set its tack on a pole or boom, but instead, fasten it on deck. Often, a tackle will be spliced to the tack and if it's completely loose, you can set the chute at one or two metres above deck level. Its shape will then become even fuller and the deepest point will wander aft. If the wind is light and the boat is sailing on a reach, you can generate more power in the sail this way.

If the wind freshens, you can take in the luff with the tackle and slightly flatten the profile to reduce heeling. It's easy to trim the luff from the cockpit if the hauling part of the tackle is led aft. Since the chute is set without a pole or boom, it's easier to handle. Downwind, on the other hand, you have less scope to set the sail clear of the blanketing effect of the main. On a run dead before the wind it might even be better to take down the main altogether or at least to reef it in order to make better use of the chute.

Some sail-makers suggest you boom it out at the clew to stop it from collapsing. While this might well be a good idea, in my view, if you're prepared to go to all that trouble you might just as well set a proper spinnaker in the first place.

The chute will also work on a shy reach and, in this respect, is superior to the spinnaker. In light winds it's also

THE SNUFFER

Today, several systems are available for lowering the spinnaker – all designed to help aleviate the stress of taking down large downwind sails. They normally consist of a nylon tube the length of the luff of the sail. Its lower opening has a GRP collar, with its largest opening towards the sail, and which swallows the sail before it's taken down. They're known as snuffers.

You set the spinnaker or cruising chute by hoisting the entire length of the tube with the sail coiled up inside. Tack and clew are pulled out of the tube at the bottom end and the sheets are bent on. Finally, the collar of the tube is pulled up towards the top of the mast with a special outhaul, after which the sail is free to unfold.

When taking in the sail, you loosen the sheet and, at the same time, haul the collar downwards until the entire sail is back in the tube. Only then is the hose taken down – and compared to pulling a huge, wildly flogging spinnaker below decks that's extremely easy. Most problems encountered with spinnakers or other large downwind sails are connected to hoisting or recovery. A tube like this is a real help here and particularly convenient on a cruising yacht with a small crew.

▲ A snuffer can be a great help and make taking down a spinnaker or blister much easier.

more effective than the genoa up to 60 degrees off the wind because of its large area and the overlap of about 170 per cent. You flatten the profile of the cruising chute on these points of sail by tightening the luff until the tack is no more than 50 or 60 centimetres above deck level.

Because the blister or chute is cut asymmetrically, it's sailed and handled like a genoa with two sheets at the clew. You can both tack and gybe with this sail, although tacking will cause it a great deal of stress. It's far better to gybe it. In order to do that, first gybe the main until the chute collapses in the lee of the main. Then shift the sail to the new side and trim it again.

The cruising chute is set like a spinnaker on its own halyard which has to run in a loose block from the mast, rather than through a fixed sheave. That's because the head of the sail moves about considerably and the halyard would quickly chafe through.

Asymmetric spinnaker or gennaker

As the name implies, this is a cross between a spinnaker and genoa. It's cut asymmetrically like a blister or cruising chute and also sheeted the same way, but its area is about the same size as a spinnaker. The tack of the asymmetric is flown from the end of a pole just like a spinnaker, but the pole itself looks more like an ancient bowsprit and protrudes from the bows. Modern asymmetric poles are often housed in laminated tubes

▲ *Some production boats like this Danish Buhl 111 for example have an asymmetric spinnaker pole fitted as standard.*

which lead below decks and can be retracted. Sometimes, they can also be swung from side to side so you can get the asymmetric away from the blanketing zone of the mainsail. That, along with its sheer size, means the asymmetric is considerably more effective than a cruising chute. On the other hand, an asymmetric is easier to set.

Because of its cut, an asymmetric is most effective on a reach, rather than dead downwind. But if you decide to gybe downwind, an asymmetric will help you cover your ground as quickly as if you were sailing dead downwind with a spinnaker. It's possible to fit a pole to your boat at a later date but if you want a retractable one, it can be quite difficult.

The question you need to ask is whether it's really worth the effort, bearing in mind the other alternative is a conventional spinnaker. However, there are quite a few production boats on the market that come with asymmetric poles as standard.

Quick reference guide

Over time, most of the rules about sail trim you've learnt on the previous pages will become second nature. When sailing, your thinking will be instinctive and so with little in the way of conscious thought you'll find you'll be able to trim your sails to achieve the best possible relationship between lift and drag on each course and in every wind strength. To that extent it's a bit like driving a car. After a while all the lessons you had become absorbed into a series of virtually automatic responses.

As a quick reference, here's an abbreviated summary:

Light wind, no waves

Upwind
To maximise lift and reduce drag without minimising it.

Mast bend: None

Headsail:
- Reduce tension on halyard
- Loosen sheet
- Move lead block forward (reduces twist)
- Check that tell-tales stream aft both to windward and leeward

Mainsail:
- Loosen backstay and, if applicable, running backstays
- Loosen trimstays if applicable
- Reduce halyard tension
- Loosen Cunningham
- Reduce foot tension
- Traveller to windward
- Open leech by reducing sheet tension
- Check that kicking strap is loose

Reaching
For lots of lift while accepting increase in drag.

Mast bend: None

Headsail:
- Reduce halyard tension
- Loosen sheet further
- Move sheet lead further forward and, if possible, outboard
- Check that tell-tales flow aft both to windward and leeward

Mainsail:
- Backstay and running backstays as loose as possible
- Trimstays loose
- No tension on halyards (no creases in sail)
- Cunningham loose
- Foot loose and open

- Open leech by reducing sheet tension
- Traveller to windward
- Introduce some tension on kicking strap

Light wind, some swell

Upwind
Aim for maximum lift, accepting obvious penalties.

Mast bend: None

Headsail:
- As little as possible halyard tension
- Sheet as loose as possible
- Sheet leads forward (less twist)
- Tell-tales streaming aft both to windward and leeward

Mainsail:
- Backstay and running backstays very loose
- Trimstays loose
- Halyard tension as little as possible
- Cunningham loose
- Open leech by easing sheet
- Traveller to windward
- Kicking strap loose

Reaching
More lift; more drag.

Mast bend: None

Headsail:
- As little as possible halyard tension
- Sheet as loose as possible
- Sheet lead further forward and if possible outboard

- Check that tell-tales stream aft both to windward and leeward.

Mainsail:
- Backstay and running backstays very loose
- Trimstays loose
- Halyard tension as little as possible
- Cunningham loose
- Open leech by easing sheet
- Traveller to windward
- Kicking strap loose

Medium wind, small waves

Upwind
Aim for best possible gliding factor, meaning as much lift and as little drag as possible.

Mast bend: Curved slightly aft

Headsail:
- Increase halyard tension
- Sheet in hard
- Sheet lead in middle position
- Tell-tales streaming aft to leeward and rising from time to time to windward

Mainsail:
- Tighten backstay and running backstays
- Tighten trimstays a little
- Increase halyard tension
- Take in Cunningham a little
- Tension foot of sail
- Traveller amidships
- Close leech by applying maximum sheet tension

- Tension kicking strap.

Reaching

More lift, increasing drag.

Mast bend: None

Headsail:
- Reduce halyard tension
- Loosen sheet
- Move sheet lead further forward and outboard
- Tell-tales streaming aft both to windward and leeward

Mainsail:
- Loosen backstay and running backstays a little
- Loosen trimstays
- Reduce halyard tension
- Reduce foot tension a bit
- Move traveller a little to leeward
- Close leech with sheet
- Tighten kicking strap

Medium wind, medium seas

Upwind

For best possible gliding factor, meaning as much lift and as little drag as possible.

Mast bend: curved slightly aft

Headsail:
- Increase halyard tension
- Sheet as tight as possible
- Sheet leads in middle position

- Tell-tales streaming aft to leeward and rising from time to time to windward

Mainsail:
- Tighten backstay and running backstays
- Tighten trimstays a little
- Increase halyard tension
- Tension Cunningham
- Tension foot of sail
- Traveller amidships
- Close leech with maximum sheet tension
- Tension kicking strap

Reaching

For more lift but increasing drag.

Mast bend: None

Headsail:
- Reduce halyard tension
- Loosen sheet
- Move sheet lead further forward and outboard
- Tell-tales streaming aft both to windward and leeward

Mainsail:
- Loosen backstay and running backstays a little
- Loosen trimstays
- Reduce halyard tension
- Loosen Cunningham
- Reduce foot tension a little
- Traveller slightly to leeward
- Close leech with sheet
- Tighten kicking strap

Strong winds

Upwind
To minimise drag, accepting reduced lift.

Mast bend: Maximum

Headsail:
- Maximum halyard tension
- Sheet as tight as possible
- Sheet lead positioned further aft
- Tell-tales streaming aft to leeward and continuously rising to windward

Mainsail:
- Maximum tension on backstay and windward runner
- Loosen trimstays
- Maximum halyard tension
- Maximum tension on Cunningham
- Maximum tension on foot
- Traveller to leeward
- Open up leech by slightly reducing sheet tension
- Maximum tension on kicking strap

Reaching
For much lift and less drag.

Mast bend: Maximum curve

Headsail:
- Tighten halyard
- Loosen sheet a little
- Sheet lead positioned further forward and outboard
- Tell-tales streaming aft both to windward and leeward

Mainsail:
- Tighten backstay and windward running backstay
- Loosen trimstays
- Increase halyard tension
- Take in Cunningham
- Maximise foot tension
- Traveller completely to leeward
- Close leech by tightening sheet
- Tighten kicking strap

Glossary

▶▶▶ **A**

● *Apparent wind:* the true wind plus the wind generated by the forward movement of the boat.

● *Aspect ratio:* the relationship between height and length. A high aspect ratio would indicate a shape that was tall and narrow.

● *Astern:* aft, towards the back.

● *Asymmetric spinnaker:* a cross between a genoa and a spinnaker with a tack attached to a boom, pole or bowsprit.

▶▶▶ **B**

● *Backstay:* a supporting wire attached to the top of the mast and fastened to the after end of the boat.

● *Barber-hauler:* block and tackle used to tension a sheet by pulling it inboard.

● *Batten:* a bendy strip used to stiffen the shape of a sail.

● *Bear away:* steer away from the wind.

● *Beat, to:* sailing towards the wind.

● *Belay:* attach and make secure.

● *Bend:* (a line in place) attach.

● *Block:* a wheel or pulley usually with an outer casing.

● *Block and tackle:* a system of wires and pulleys.

▶▶▶ **C**

● *Catboat:* usually a boat with a mast stepped in the bows and no headsail.

● *Centre of effort:* the geometrical mid-point of a sail.

● *Centre of lateral resistance:* the geometrical mid-point of the boat's underwater profile.

● *Centreboard:* a retractable device which provides grip, like a keel.

● *Circulation:* a circular flow around a body triggered by the initial or starter vortex.

● *Clew:* a point where the foot of a sail meets the leech.

● *Close hauled:* sailing to windward with the sheets pulled in tight.

● *Cruising chute:* a full-bodied headsail used for running or reaching, usually without a boom or pole.

● *Cunningham:* a line controlling the luff tension of sails.

● *Cutter:* rig with two headsails, jib and staysail.

▶▶▶ **D**

● *Dead before the wind:* with the wind right behind.

● *Displacement:* the weight of water displaced by the boat which equates to the weight of the boat.

● *Displacement speed:* the maximum speed a boat can move through the water without planing.

● *Downhaul:* a line used to pull down a sail.

▶▶▶ **F**

● *Foot:* the bottom edge of a sail.

● *Forestay:* a supporting wire attached to the mast and a point on or near the bows.

Fractional rig: a rig where the headsail is attached to a stay which terminates a fraction of the way down from the top of the rig.

▶▶▶ G

Genoa: a large overlapping headsail.

Gliding factor: a coefficient denoting the degree of lift over drag. The higher the number, the greater the lift.

Guy: a control line attached to a spinnaker pole.

Gybe, to: altering direction with the wind astern so the boom changes sides.

▶▶▶ H

Halyard: a rope or wire used to hoist a sail.

Head: the top part of a sail.

Headsail furling: revolving mechanism used to reef or roll up a headsail.

Heeling: when a boat leans over due to the force of the wind.

▶▶▶ I

In-boom reefing: a mechanism which winds the foot of the mainsail into the boom, reducing its area.

In-mast reefing: a mechanism which winds the mainsail into the mast, reducing its area.

▶▶▶ J

Jet theory: sometimes referred to as the Venturi or slot effect which analyses the way the gap between overlapping sails speeds up the flow and affects performance.

Jib: the outermost headsail.

Jib boom: a spar attached to the clew of a headsail.

▶▶▶ K

Keel: an appendage attached to the bottom of a boat to provide stability and grip.

Ketch: two-masted rig with smaller mizzen sail aft.

Kicker/kicking strap or boom vang: a device used to pull the boom down.

▶▶▶ L

Laminar flow: a layered stream flowing in one direction.

Lee: the opposite side from which the wind is blowing.

Lee helm: when a boat tries to turn away from the wind when sailing to windward.

Leech: the after edge of a sail.

Leeway: degree of sideways movement when sailing to windward.

Lift: a positive perpendicular force which acts on a sail, wing or aerofoil.

Luff: the front edge of a sail.

Luff up: head into the wind.

▶▶▶ M

Mast rake: the angle a mast makes with the perpendicular.

Masthead rig: a rig where the headsail is attached to a stay which terminates at the top of the mast.

Mizzen: after sail in a two-masted rig.

▶▶▶ O

Outhaul: a line commonly used to pull the clew of a sail along a boom.

▶▶▶ P

Parasail: a wing-shaped sail designed to lighten the bows of a boat when running under the spinnaker.

Pitch: the up and down motion of a boat in a swell.

▶ ▶ ▶ **R**

- *Radial head spinnaker:* a spinnaker with panels radiating out from the head.
- *Reaching:* sailing with the wind on or forward of the beam.
- *Reef down:* reduce sail area.
- *Resistance:* a force acting like a brake, operating in the same direction as the flow.
- *Rudder:* a hinged steering device attached to the after end of a boat.
- *Running backstays:* additional wire supports attached to the mast and secured aft which have to be alternatively slackened or tensioned on each tack.
- *Running rigging:* ropes or wires used to raise or lower sails.

▶ ▶ ▶ **S**

- *Schooner:* two-masted rig with larger sail aft.
- *Sheet:* a line attached to the clew of a sail.
- *Shroud:* standing rigging that supports the mast laterally.
- *Snuffer:* a tube designed to facilitate spinnaker retrieval.
- *Spreaders/crosstrees:* horizontal struts attached to the mast which tension the thrust of the shrouds.
- *Stagnation point:* where a flow separates in different directions.
- *Standing rigging:* wires supporting the mast.
- *Starter vortex:* an eddy created by the stream acting on a body which drives a circular motion
- *Storm jib:* a small, tough, heavy-weather headsail.
- *Storm trysail:* a small, tough, heavy sail usually set flying in stormy weather instead of the mainsail.

▶ ▶ ▶ **T**

- *Tack:* to turn the bows of the boat through the eye of the wind when sailing to windward.
- *Tack:* where the luff of a sail meets the foot.
- *Tear off edge:* where a laminar airflow breaks away.
- *Tell-tales:* ribbons, yarn or tape etc attached to the sail to indicate wind flow.
- *Topping lift:* a line supporting the boom.
- *Traveller:* a sliding mechanical device used to change the mainsheet's angle of pull.
- *Tri-radial spinnaker:* a spinnaker with panels radiating out from all three corners.
- *Twist:* the change in a sail's shape in the vertical plane.

▶ ▶ ▶ **V**

- *Vortex:* a swirling mass.

▶ ▶ ▶ **W**

- *Weather helm:* when a boat tries to round up towards the wind when sailing to windward.
- *Wind abeam:* the wind on the side of the boat.
- *Windward:* towards the wind.

▶ ▶ ▶ **Y**

- *Yaw, to:* slewing from side to side.
- *Yawl:* two-masted rig similar to ketch but with relatively smaller mizzen sail aft.

Index